Matthew 'Ollie' Ollerton is a
author and a former Special F
the founding Directing Staff o
Who Dares Wins and *SAS Austr*

Ollie's military career began at the age of 18 when he joined the Royal Marine Commandos and toured operationally in Northern Ireland and in Iraq for Operation Desert Storm. He subsequently spent six years in the Special Boat Service rising to team leader, before working in Iraq as a private security contractor and carrying out anti-child-trafficking charity work in Southeast Asia. These experiences helped shape his life as well as his books.

Ollie is the founder of Breakpoint, the business he runs as part of his mission to help others create more productive, healthier, and happier lives. He furthers this passion through his writing and his online, virtual and public appearances.

OLLIE OLLERTON

HOW TO SURVIVE *almost* ANYTHING

THE SPECIAL FORCES GUIDE TO STAYING ALIVE

bl!nk

First published in the UK in 2025 by Blink Publishing
An imprint of Bonnier Books UK
5th Floor, HYLO, 105 Bunhill Row,
London, EC1Y 8LZ

A CIP catalogue record for this book is available from the British Library.

Paperback ISBN: 9781788705028
Hardback ISBN: 9781788704984
Trade Paperback ISBN: 9781788704991

Also available as an ebook and an audiobook

1 3 5 7 9 10 8 6 4 2

Design and Typeset by Envy Design Ltd

Illustrations: 11, 29, 45, 103, 167, 185, 251 & header icons – © Shutterstock
32, 38, 40, 42, 55–65, 69, 82, 92, 177 – Envy Design Ltd

Printed and bound in Great Britain by Clays Ltd, Elcograf S.p.A.

MIX
Paper | Supporting responsible forestry
FSC® C018072
FSC www.fsc.org

The authorised representative in the EEA is
Bonnier Books UK (Ireland) Limited.
Registered office address: Floor 3, Block 3, Miesian Plaza,
Dublin 2, D02 Y754, Ireland
compliance@bonnierbooks.ie

www.bonnierbooks.co.uk

CONTENTS

A NOTE FROM THE AUTHOR

My name is Ollie Ollerton. I am a survivor, a former UK Special Forces soldier and, at the time of writing this book, have 51 years of experience on this planet. I have been trained to fight and survive in every known theatre of operations, from jungle to arctic, desert to sea. My purpose in writing this book is to prepare you for various scenarios that could happen to any of us. It's not rocket science and I don't consider myself an expert. What I do consider myself to be is a self-aware human who values highly the ability to think in a rational and practical manner, with the knowledge and experience to handle any given situation that I may find myself in. I want to share that knowledge with you as it could very well save your life, or someone else's for that matter. The last thing anyone wants to die of is ignorance, so well done for taking the first step towards an education you cannot afford not to have.

INTRODUCTION

A person who knows bad things are coming their way but continues to ignore that reality is someone not in charge of their life. Like the person who doesn't set any money aside for emergencies – a new boiler or clutch for their car – and when this unexpected payment is required, they then can't pay their regular bills. If you're thinking to yourself, *that's me!* don't worry, you're not in the minority. And, believe it or not, I was that person too in days gone by! So many of us have got used to just getting by and living on a prayer that nothing will go wrong. And yet we know full well that things go wrong on a regular basis, that's life, and expecting anything different is crazy; it's really just a matter of time before you get curveballed.

Sometimes, we only realise how lucky we were yesterday when something really unpleasant lands in our lap today. A part of me believes that while certain events in life happen for a reason – one door closing so another can open, or a powerful lesson needing to be learnt before we can move on and evolve – for all of that, there are so many needless tragedies that occur without any meaning. Things that are utterly random and have no silver lining, like one of our siblings gets cancer, or a dear friend is hit by a car. Life can feel unspeakably cruel when sod's law seems to be working against you.

I don't believe for a moment that something is actively working against you, but I do believe that we can try to master our mindset so it's a positive one. The vibration you give out to the universe is what you will receive back. Out there, the universe is a big, unpredictable place. There are wormholes and black holes, meteors fly through it on their trajectory and can crash into anything in their path. And yet there are still things which you can control, take responsibility for, be on top of and anticipate.

When we unconsciously focus on a fear of something – let's say losing our job, or being mugged or bullied – by thinking about it again and again we invite it to ourselves. What you focus your attention on comes to you, that's the rule of the universe. But it's never too late to get prepared, to start facing down your fears and getting ready for them, because otherwise these gremlins have a way of searching you out, putting you on the spot and testing you. Until we prepare to meet our worst fears head-on, they will never go away and will forever keep knocking at our door. If you're haunted by the constant anxiety of being beaten up each time you leave your front door, it's time you got yourself on a self-defence course, after which, with your improved confidence, because you now know you can deal with the situation, it's likely it will never happen. Perhaps more importantly, that anxiety that you've been carrying around will go away and stop irking you.

Remember, good or bad, conscious or unconscious, it's what you focus on in life that you draw towards you. There's a massive difference between realistic positive thinking and that delusional, lazy state of hopefulness where you believe you'll never get ill or you don't need to put aside money for a pension because you're going to win the next *Britain's Got Talent*; positive thinking is built on intention and following it with action, while delusional thinking is fuelled by fantasy, self-denial and inertia.

There will always be challenges – isn't that what life is all about? To grow, we need to embrace these difficulties, constantly pushing ourselves out of the known into the unknown. We must tackle fresh things and constantly learn, finessing the way we go about things we already know. So don't go at it blind – do your prep. If you're going hiking in the Rocky Mountains, where you'll be sharing the landscape with grizzly bears, cougars and unpredictable weather, you'll need a knife, map, bear repellent, bags to seal up your food, a warm waterproof coat and access to running water. You'll need to consider the drop in temperature at night, ensuring you are adequately insulated with a decent sleeping bag, and you'll require a compass, phone with GPS, the National Park's emergency number and, of course, a basic medical kit. You'll also need to let people know where you're going. With this squared away, you are now in a position to enjoy yourself in the knowledge that unless you're abducted by aliens, gored by an elk or hassled by Sasquatch, your basic curveballs are sorted. (Yes, we'll get to grizzlies a little later!)

Writing this, the sunburn I got while summiting one of the most technical climbs in the Himalayas, Ama Dablam, a 6,812-metre mountain in Nepal, is still burning my cheeks. This climb perfectly illustrates the need to prep for and be ready to deal with potential disasters. If we had just plunged into the expedition without knowledgeable porters, the right gear and a climb leader who had the experience to get us up and down the mountain, the chances that we would have failed, or I wouldn't even be here to write this, are pretty huge.

Before I travelled to Nepal, I paid a visit to the altitude chamber at the sports and science department of Manchester Metropolitan University. I wanted to make sure that I had a good level of fitness, that my 51-year-old body was up to the challenge the Himalayas would present, otherwise the experience could become a trauma rather than a joy. So at the university, they tested my VO2 max (volume, oxygen, maximum), the optimum rate at which my heart, lungs and muscles use oxygen during exercise, to see how well I recovered at altitude. I exercised on a bike and on a treadmill with a backpack while they monitored me and I was more than happy to hear that I had the cardio capacity of a 30-year-old!

We couldn't just charge up Ama Dablam; we had to acclimatise ourselves to her rarefied air for a few days beforehand, adjusting to the lower levels of oxygen at high altitude. The higher you climb, the harder it is for your body to get oxygen around your body. Your heart rate goes up so you have to breathe faster and faster; eventually, even walking becomes tiring. To deal with the lack of oxygen, your blood vessels tighten up. This means an increase of pressure, which can lead to them bursting, flooding your lungs and brain with blood. So, in order to prepare our bodies, we had to climb to camp two and then come down to the base camp again. Only then were we ready to go for the summit. Slowgress is progress!

It was only by getting all our ducks in a row that we were able to thrive in the moment and enjoy the climb. We did our prep and tried to keep out of the path of disaster as much as we possibly could. Once we'd done all we could, the rest was up to chance.

When I was in the British Special Forces, before we were dropped into a mission, we minimised things that might go wrong by being as thoroughly prepped as possible, including studying the intel on our target and anticipating their response. We considered every detail we could think of that might make the difference between taking our last breath or returning in one piece. How many unfriendlies were there? Where was the entrance and exit?

What level of arsenal might our target fight back with? Directly after a mission and no matter how exhausted we were, we had a debrief in which we discussed our weaknesses, what went well and what didn't go well . . . constantly asking ourselves if we could have prepped even better. Preparation is the key to survival.

To be prepared is to give yourself a chance to thrive. For me, whether it's running a business or responding to an emergency, this is about being ready for and resilient to the storms that can and probably will beat at your door. And because of your foresight, where others perish, you will survive and even thrive. Awareness and preparation allow you to be at your strongest because by anticipating what's coming at you, you can position yourself with an adequate response. As the old saying goes, 'I'm not looking for trouble but if it knocks at my door, it will find me very much at home (and ready!)'. It's not about doom-mongering, it's a case of being realistic and considering the odds of what could go wrong.

Sometime after I left the Special Boat Service, I found my true purpose in the Far East, helping to extract and save young children from a hellish life they had been committed to in the sex trade. It was much more dangerous than the SBS work because I had no firepower whatsoever and no muckers to back me up, never mind the luxury of being able to call in an aerial assault using millions of pounds worth of tech that would unleash fury. But for a forward rendezvous point with the rest of the team, I was on my own. If anything went tits up, well, that was on me.

But the worst problem was these interventions were barely prepped and intel was scant. I'd often enter hostile territory – the camps where the young children were kept – without any firm knowledge of the layout of cells or the number of hostiles, etc. Once I was in, I was scoping what I had to do as surreptitiously as possible on the spot. And every den had a wolf pimp guarding it, in this case 'captive', cubs. It was living by your wits and while I was happy to roll that way because of the cause, I knew from experience that my chances of survival lay in forward planning, not by flying by the now-threadbare seat of my pants. Sometimes we just don't have the luxury of time, but when we do have it, we're crazy not to use it and shut the gate *before* the horse bolts.

This book is about taking control of yourself and adapting to your environment, *any* environment: whether it's a world that is overheating, becoming frozen or disappearing in floodwater; be it an earthquake, nuclear war or societal collapse. No plan survives first contact goes the saying and, agreed, you can't control everything. But you can at least prepare for these spectres that could harm you and your family. The more we learn to look after ourselves, the closer we get to feeling prep-fit and ready, common sense switched on, alarm snooze turned off!

So, who is this book for? Run-for-the-hills-type nut jobs, survivalists and doomsaying pessimists? No, it's for you, the average person. You don't have to believe that the earth is flat or that humankind has never walked on the moon to be someone who prepares for potentially drastic conditions – just someone who is aware of the dangers that can impact our lives and wants to do something to get ready for highly likely future scenarios. I guarantee you will sleep easier having read the advice in these pages, much of it gained first hand in desert, jungle and arctic survival training during my time as a Special Forces soldier.

How likely are the scenarios in this book to happen? We are in truth one rogue nuke, one sudden shift in temperature, one charismatic upstart creating political freefall and turning us against the establishment away from losing the equilibrium we take for granted. What can't be ignored is the acceleration of the number and severity of disasters in our natural world – for example, extreme droughts, extreme temperatures and mudslides are all on the rise – and the effects on us humans are going to be myriad as events become more difficult to manage. Helping the next person is in our DNA and lets our best side shine, but we must be equipped to deal with the worst of human nature as well. This book will prepare you for (almost) any scenario you're likely to face – whether that's arming you with the essential skills to head out and thrive in the wilderness, fight off aggressive animals or be one step ahead when society breaks down, you'll have the knowledge to be confident that you're ready for whatever life throws at you.

Ollie Ollerton

Somewhere in the Western Hemisphere, 2023

HOW TO USE THIS BOOK

This book is easily navigable as it's split into easy-to-access sections starting with the **Survivor's Mindset.** Before we do anything, we need to become accustomed to the mental state that is needed to survive and thrive. Once we've mastered this mindset, we move onto the **Essentials**, which details how to plan ahead, the kit and skills you'll need to acquire, how to stay warm and dry, and administer first aid. The obstacles to survive have been split up in **Part Three** as we discuss **Climate and Terrain**, which explores the dangers caused by the earth itself. Following this is **Personal Crises**, which looks at how to deal with things which can suddenly turn our lives upside down, like the loss of a loved one, addiction or job loss. **Part Five** discusses **Aggression**, looking at attacks to your person, be it from a wild animal or a human. Finally, there's the **Breakdown of Society**, which is caused by people and encompasses anything from a biochemical attack to a nuclear war.

PART ONE:

THE SURVIVOR'S MINDSET

WHAT MAKES A SURVIVOR?

Is it somebody who is lucky or somebody who is determined not to be beaten, whatever the odds are against them? When, for the second and final time, I was attempting to pass 'Selection', the gruelling six-month test to gain entry into the elite Special Boat Service, towards the end of the process I suffered a broken ankle and had to tape it up to finish; I would not be beaten by it, despite the staff and a doctor telling me it was over.

Survival is rarely an accident; there is a reason some people find the necessary grit in themselves to stand up and face a really challenging situation and why others just give up. We all have a drive to survive, but in some it's stronger than others. Take Frenchman Henri Charrière, better known as Papillon, who was wrongly accused of murder and shipped out to the penal colony of French Guiana for life imprisonment. Driven by his desire for revenge against the judge who wrongfully condemned him, he escaped a staggering 13 times, even from the Devil's Island, a previously inescapable prison.

Survivors don't have time to be a victim, nor is there any room for blaming others or entertaining self-defeating beliefs, like the universe is out to get them. When they find themselves in a challenging situation their focus is on accepting what's happening, adapting to that environment and staying positive. If you can smile, however grimly, and keep a sense of humour you're halfway there. The difference between those who can endure and those who can't is self-belief and fortitude of mind. When you believe you can make it then every step you take brings you closer to that goal. Of course, the harder things get, the more that unhelpful inner voice will surface, the one that says, 'I want to rest now', 'I'm too scared to go forward', 'I'll just have a sleep . . .' You must fight that urge and adapt to the situation.

Many of you will be natural survivors; you'll already possess that inner grit that will keep you going till the end. And if you don't think you have it, maybe you've never been really tested before. During Selection, I noticed that it wasn't the meatheads who got through to the final stages, instead it was those who were mentally muscular. There was a look of determination in their eyes, they just got on with it.

In his masterpiece *Man's Search for Meaning*, Jewish psychiatrist Viktor Frankl describes first-hand the brutality he experienced in a Nazi concentration camp. Having lost most of his family to the gas chambers he could so easily have given up, but instead he challenged himself to become a better person. Frankl noticed that those prisoners who operated from a place of purpose, love and respect towards others, as well as those who found courage in themselves even under these near-intolerable conditions, survived the longest. They found meaning in themselves through helping others. He also noted that physically – like the lads who made it through Selection – it wasn't the muscular specimens who prevailed in the long run, but those who had a sense of purpose, who refused to sink to the bestial level of their incarceration. And then there were those who kept themselves alive with the hope that they would one day see their loved ones again. They visualised it in their minds, which gave them something to live for.

Visualise success. Hope for the best but prepare for the worst. Self-doubt is caused by looking to control things which are beyond your control, like your past or the actions of others. Acceptance of what's happened and understanding that you cannot control another person, at the same time as taking responsibility for your actions, is the start of true self-possession. If we focus on negatives, we just draw negatives back to us. When we tell ourselves what we're going to do and have a strong reason *why* we are doing it, it's amazing how much we can achieve.

Humans are built for survival. We have prevailed over hundreds of thousands of years by being very selective with the battles we fight and the ones we flee from. When we are under threat our pupils dilate and our vision narrows in order that we can focus clearly on the perceived threat and make the right decision to run or fight.

The chemical reactions in our brain help us to react quickly and survive, but it's also what you tell yourself that propels you to safety or not. In a dangerous or life-threatening situation, tell yourself your ultimate aim is to survive, you are going to make it, then allow yourself to work backwards from that. Ask yourself what the number-one threat is here that you're dealing with, then plan how to handle it. If you're banking on a quick fix, be prepared to alter that expectation when things go wrong. It's better to prepare your mind for the long run. Again, no plan ever survives first contact – your initial response is merely a rough blueprint on which to build. A true survivor is adept at prioritising what needs to be done first in an emergency and remains ever ready to adapt and switch tack as needed when first approaches don't work out. We've got to be a situational chameleon.

EMBRACE CHANGE

Up until 15,000 years ago, we humans were still being hunted for food. Cavemen didn't pop out of their caves in the morning and think about the content they would put on their Insta reel that day, where they could get their latte from or whether they should get out and do some networking to increase their personal market value! No, they just wanted to know what could kill them, where it was likely to come from and to make sure they had the right weapons to get the upper hand in order to prevail. We became top of the food chain through the fact we had – and still have – things that animals don't, such as will, intellect, reason, imagination, intuition, memory and perception.

Humanity is the weakest it's ever been. Come the day when we are faced with any form of disaster, whether that's personal or on a larger scale, unless we toughen up, many of us will fall to pieces and hide inside our cocoon of limitation and victim mindset. But we mustn't remain glued to the spot and stagnant, diligently in place waiting for the environment to change before we do. We must be the situational chameleon, not focused on the past or living in fear of the future, but instead challenging habitual behaviour to adapt and thrive. Try to embrace the discomfort of change, trusting that it will lead you to a more desirable circumstance or environment.

LETTING GO OF TRAUMA

I am a survivor. The memory of the chimp attack that almost took my life as a boy lurks in the shadows of my mind like a grotesque nightmare. You force yourself to wake up, reassuring yourself that 'it was just a dream'. I used to repeat this to myself over and over. But it wasn't; it actually happened to me at the age of ten and the trauma it caused was something that riddled my life with addiction and hardship. I only dealt with this many-horned nemesis a few years ago, 39 years after the event took place.

If you've read *Battle Ready* or *Break Point*, you'll be familiar with what happened. One hot day one summer the circus came to the Staffordshire town where I lived. My brother and I wandered around backstage, free to roam from one animal enclosure to the next. In a grassy clearing surrounded by tents, I spotted one of the most adorable little creatures I'd ever seen (don't tell my dog Murphy, he'll get jealous!). The baby chimp was chained to a post, eating some fruit, chattering away, and offered me half a banana. I was completely entranced but then his mother appeared from nowhere and flew at me with bared teeth, her eyes hot with hatred. It all happened very quickly from here on as she knocked me back with her immense weight and buried her canines into my forearms, which I was trying to block my face with. Everything turned red and through the cracks in my fingers, I saw strings of bloody viscera hanging from her mouth. *My* viscera.

There's something that happens to herbivores when attacked by a predator. After the initial attempt to escape the pursued simply give up and allow themselves to be eaten while they're still alive. You see it again and again on wildlife documentaries. The creature gave it its best shot and now capitulates without a fuss. But humans don't give up so easily, we have a spirit of individuality within us and we are hardwired to survive.

Yes, I was petrified but something inside me clicked, something old and primal that told me I was not going to allow myself to be ripped apart and that I must do my damnedest to get this monster off my chest. I kicked back with all my strength. My feet connected with the chimp's chest, overturning the surprised monkey, who fell backwards. I then scrambled as far out of the way as I could. But before I knew it, she was charging at me for the second time on all fours, those yellow fangs now coated in blood. There must have been a god looking down that day because just as she was so close that I could smell her acrid breath, and knew this time it was curtains, her collar suddenly yanked brutally at her neck as she reached the chain's extremity. I was out of her range by just a few inches. She was screaming with rage.

Later in life, with the help of the ayahuasca plant and a shaman who helped guide me through nightmare visions of the attack, I learnt to accept that the chimp was doing what her DNA programmed her to do – protect her young. She did what any parent would do if such a threat posed itself, sacrificing her own well-being to eliminate that threat. I barely escaped with my life, the value of which I have only just recently started to appreciate after myriad mental traumas that have haunted me for most of my days.

The truth is we are all survivors. You may not know it, but when you're pinned into a corner, your life balancing on a knife's edge, a primal instinct and an inner strength will prevail. Like the mother chimp, the strongest reactions are driven by our desire to survive and to protect our species at all costs.

This is where I consider our biggest conflict exists. On one side, we have our survival blueprint trying to keep us safe and on the other, our soul yearns for experience, adventure, for us to take risks and get the most from life.

Our instinct to survive by the easiest means would be content with us hiding in a dark corner, fed and watered, procreating as much as possible. As far as our species is concerned, we are here not to discover other worlds and celebrate life, but to create more humans. Do you think your survival mindset wants you to jump out of planes, ride fast motorbikes and climb mountains? One hundred per cent not and this is where the inner battle starts. We are more naturally driven to survive at a basic, safe and modest level, and that's why so many of us are happy to rub along in 'comfort zones' that offer no real comfort, no growth whatsoever.

Have you ever been to an event where you are introduced to people you haven't met before and straight after the handshake you have no idea of the names of those who you've just shaken hands with? Yes, is the answer! The reason for this is that your mind is scanning for threat, it is going into its memory banks of previous image captures to find if it has met that person before, and then to match the image with the emotion, good or bad. So, when there is no match, your mind is on high alert and names are well down the list of priorities. This works the same for new experiences and is the reason most of us turn away from anything like taking a step towards uncharted territory.

The safe survival mind wants us to keep on doing what we did yesterday and the day before that and so on, as it's familiar, regardless of whether it's a good or bad experience. It just wants to repeat the habit that allows us to stay alive. The mind adores repetition – this goes back to our very first days of finding a food and a water source. Once we had found it, we kept returning to the same location, consuming the same food source and water that offered no threat and kept us surviving. It's up to us to actively break this cycle and embrace experiences that are out of our comfort zone.

A SPIRIT OF ADVENTURE

Maybe you are in your teens and you feel like your parent isn't as active as they, or you for that matter, would like them to be. Perhaps you want to help them out of this rut or get to know them for the first time as you approach adulthood. Or maybe that parent is you and you want to shake yourself up, get yourself fit and learn how to survive in the wilderness. Or is it that you want to encourage your child to reduce their screen time for a few days and come on an adventure with you? A long time ago, parents and children spent more time together, when children were taught hunting and other skills. I'm sure you remember from your own experience that growing up as a teenager is all about finding your own tribe, but as a parent wouldn't it be great to enjoy occasional adventures together again and learn new things? To subtly prove to them there is life beyond social media and that phone, seemingly grafted to his hand.

It doesn't matter whether you're sat on a Shropshire hill looking up at the Big Dipper or you are regarding the same constellation up a mountain in Nepal, in both cases you are connecting with something bigger than yourself – dare I say it, something *universal*, and it is the spirit of adventure that carried you there. Looking at those stars dotted about the blackness of space like diamonds on a jeweller's cloth, you know they were there long before you arrived and will be for long afterwards.

There's nothing more boring than living forever (name me one happy vampire!) and mankind's delight should be that his life is actually very short – the perfect length, in fact, to seek out adventure and experiences that give meaning through special moments where, in the briefest of glimpses, you can see that, like a celestial spider's web, everything is connected. We can do anything; we can create our own adventure. Man's curse is that he so often realises all this much too late in his brief tenure of time. What I want to do is to instil in you this spirit of adventure, embracing it not just when you're on your annual holiday or a backpacking trip but building it into your daily life.

Steve Jobs, the co-founder of Apple, famously said: 'Remembering that I'll be dead soon is the most important tool I've ever encountered to help me make big choices in life. Because of almost everything – all external expectations all pride, all fear of embarrassment or failure – these things just fall away in the face of death, leaving only what is truly important. Remembering that you are going to die is the best way I know to avoid the trap of thinking that you have something to lose. You are already naked. There is no reason not to follow your heart.'

How can two people with a similar start in life have such different experiences? The answer is your outlook. One person focuses on the microscopic, gets caught on the treadmill of days and weeks and lives up to Henry Thoreau's approximation that 'most men live lives of quiet desperation'; while the other seeks the unknown and stays open to the moment, faithful to the *now*. This spirit of enquiry leads this person up hills on a starlit night, gets them up in the dark to catch the dawn surf and allows them to picture themselves doing things other people can only dream of. The spirit of adventure breathes courage into someone with this mentality to dare to want to put their stamp on life, become a bigger version of themself and reach their inner potential.

The more you water this spirit with action, the easier it is to access the courage it takes to break out of your comfort zone. It's the breaking free of this (un)comfort(able) zone that is so difficult. The great thing is that it gets instantly easier the moment you make the decision and commit to putting your boots on, feeling the excitement of a thousand possibilities as you lace up and open the door. The first step into the unknown is already taken, tearing out all those spontaneity-killing weeds that can grow up around us when we stay still too long. When you get outdoors into nature and welcome back the spirit of adventure in yourself, like a glowing ember that roars to life, it will carry you along to the places you were supposed to see.

Remember when someone told you that 'life is not a rehearsal' and you just nodded? They were in fact sharing a divine truth with you – life is to be lived fully and cherished. Novelist Jack Kerouac said: 'In the end you won't remember how much time you spent in the office or mowing your lawn. Go climb that goddamn mountain.' So, whatever your adventure might be, start putting it into action. I think it was Ollie Ollerton, a lesser-known scribe, who once said, 'Nothing in life was ever great, unless at some point you doubted your ability to achieve it.'

HOW TO SURVIVE IN THE WILDERNESS

In order to truly embrace this spirit of adventure, you'll need to first understand the basics needed to survive your forays into the wilderness – which we'll look at in depth later as you progress through this book. Technology doesn't have to be a dirty word. In fact, GPS systems and mobile phones can be vital aids to your survival. But to really thrive in the wilderness, you need to ditch those comfort habits like Instagram or Facebook, disconnect from your usual world of noise and embrace the rugged unknown. There's no calling Uber to deliver your takeaway to the forest you're sleeping in tonight – much more satisfying is that salmon you just flyfished from a river, gutted, cleaned and are currently cooking on a skillet over the fire you made. Equally, it's not about being an absolute purist, no one will think any worse of you for taking a lighter along and a couple of firelighters.

To survive any wilderness you'll need to learn to:

- Build a fire to keep you warm, enable you to cook raw food and keep predatory animals at bay.
- Find a water source and make it potable. Given that a human can only survive without water for three days before the body starts to break down, this is your priority. To make water safe to drink you can boil it or, better still, if you have them, use iodine tablets or a water filtration system.
- Forage or hunt for food. If you've survived a plane crash in the wild you may be able to find existing supplies scattered in the vicinity. Otherwise, it is a case of hunting by using snares or fishing with an improvised rod and line.
- Make a shelter to protect you from the sun or keep you warm and dry in the cold or wet.
- Navigate. It's easy to lose yourself in unfamiliar surrounds, so knowing where you've set up camp and where you're heading is crucial.
- Keep clean. If you've sustained open wounds you need to keep them clean and regularly dressed, as they are a breeding ground for bacteria and can easily become infected, especially in the damp humidity of a jungle.

- Keep calm. A strong mindset is key to practising all the above, as if your resolve fails so will everything else. Try not to panic, as focusing on the negatives will just spin you out and this is when you'll make potentially life-threatening mistakes. Think everything through.

And along with these skills, here are five bits of survival kit you should have as an absolute bare minimum:

Cutting: blades, axes and saws

Combustion: fire-making tools, such as matches and lighters, and tinder to sustain it

Cover: a poncho, tarpaulin plastic sheeting, anything to keep you dry

Container: a vessel you can keep water in, preferably metal as it retains the temperature

Cordage: string, shoelaces, rope, belt . . . anything you can use to fasten things together.

Once you've mastered and gathered the above, you're well-placed to succeed, survive and thrive.

EMBRACING RISK AND GOING BACK TO BASICS

In the West, we have fallen into the trap of always following the trodden path and as a result, we have become sheep. Our world is a place where everything is done for us: livestock is bred and slaughtered out of sight before being cleaned, cut into pieces and sold in our supermarkets so that we are completely disassociated from the animal we eat at our dinner table. We don't prey on our food – there's no need to chase it when it's all there packaged and immaculate at the touch of a button. These days, we don't even need to move from the sofa as many of us do our shopping online and have it delivered.

We don't need to build fires as we have electricity (for the meantime!), nor do we need to run outside, as we have indoor gyms. We don't have to look at a map as we now have sat nav. We don't even need to meet somebody when it's just as easy to message or email them, or even better you can FaceTime or WhatsApp them. And dating – these days you shop for your future partner based on their photo. Bit by bit, these new luxuries are diluting rather than distilling our essence, our awareness of the earth and closeness to each other. And perhaps most importantly, they are stealing our self-dependence. Russell Means, one of the pioneers of the American Indian Movement, said: 'Without freedom life is pointless. The more dependent you become on centralised power, the more easily you are lead around.'

In most parts of the planet, you can get a pretty good signal and generally know where you are through your phone's GPS coordinates, so you don't experience the primal fear of being lost and then the satisfaction of finding your way back to a waypoint; it's all done for you. And if there's something you don't know, all you have to do is a Google search and some kind of explanation will appear.

On the surface of it, all these shortcuts we now take for granted might seem to be making life easier, but in fact they are eroding our inner resourcefulness. We are increasingly reducing ourselves to mentally blunted and physically atrophied beings who have lost the ability to do things ourselves.

Carl Jung, the Swiss psychiatrist, said: 'We may think there is a safe road but that will be the road of death when nothing happens any longer – not the right things. Anyone who takes the safe road is as good as dead.' Jung is suggesting a kind of spiritual death of the self when we keep to the trodden path. In this predictable place nothing new flourishes, the days and weeks roll into one and the soul seems to shut down. But when we take risks, we are waking ourselves up with the prospect of a reward and prising ourselves away from the familiar. When we immerse ourselves in the wilderness it's as if a light has been turned on inside of us and we start to feel more in touch with our feelings and sensory faculties. Our inner tranquillity and intuition start to come back to us and as we become more mindful of our environment, we begin to notice things that were previously overlooked.

Going back to basics for me is about paring down your choices so you're no longer bombarded by the angst of so many options. Less is more and you soon realise that nature's simple treasures are far more satisfying than anything a credit card can buy. Cooking up breakfast in a forest accompanied by the morning song of a gibbon is pure magic and beats the hell out of being served Eggs Benedict in a fancy hotel. Being in the wilderness gives you a chance to reset in the place where your ancestors came from.

Perhaps you consider going back to basics as buying a plot of land and becoming completely independent by going off-grid, growing your own food and harnessing the weather for your own electricity. Or maybe your version of going back to basics is spending one hour in every four weekends doing something immersed in nature. Whatever it is you choose to do, the more time you spend in wild places, the closer you get to yourself.

PART TWO:

ESSENTIALS

BACK TO BASICS

These early pages cover the building blocks of preparation, progressing to more demanding scenarios. 'Forewarned is forearmed' – I don't know who originally said this, but it may as well be the mantra for this book, as the more you know about what to do when faced with the dangers of extreme weather, terrain and environments, people and vicious animals, the easier it is to relax in the flow, bend with it and not fight against it. Finding your flow and going with it is the opposite of the survival blueprint where you get fixed in one place.

Imagine a man whose plane has crashed in the jungle and is being pursued by cannibals. He finds a cave for the night; it's comfy and dry, there is even some food there and a sleeping bag. No one is home so he stays one night and sleeps soundly. He even eats some of the food. His safe survival mind tells him he's hit the jackpot and if he stays here, he will have food and shelter. And so, he stays one more night in this new comfort zone, only to find himself on a spit roast when the cannibals come back to their cave, having been hunting him for the last two days and nights. Safe is not always best.

Martial arts master Bruce Lee famously taught: 'Be formless, shapeless like water. You put water into a cup, it becomes the cup. You put water into a bottle, it becomes the bottle. You put water into a teapot, it becomes the teapot. Now water can flow and it can crash. Be water, my friend.' In other words, learn to adapt to whatever situation you're placed in. Embrace it, don't resist it. Learn to flow through the cracks.

THINKING AHEAD

You wouldn't climb into a boxing ring with an opponent you knew nothing about; you'd do a bit of research on them and their style. And the same must be true of any unknown terrain in which you place yourself. To have the best chance of survival you need to go equipped with knowledge. Courage is important of course, but courage has its limitations when you're up against nature. An old man in a sailboat who can read the sea is 20 times more effective than 15 warriors in a long boat.

The Amazon jungle wasn't crossed in the first attempt, nor was Everest summited by the first mountaineer to attempt it. They both had to be done in stages. Just as a Special Forces soldier isn't made overnight. They start off as a regular British Forces soldier, then, having passed Selection, they begin a study into soldiering all over again, but on a much higher and more demanding level. As Special Forces operators, we were always learning because there are always new challenges to face, but everything is built upon the foundation and discipline of what we first learnt as young soldiers. We had to learn to do the basics really well, regardless of how tired, hungry and scared we may have been. In the same way, you need to start small if you're a novice explorer and gradually build up your survival skillset before you are ready to tackle the hard stuff.

THE WAY HUMANS WORK: MASLOW'S HIERARCHY OF NEEDS

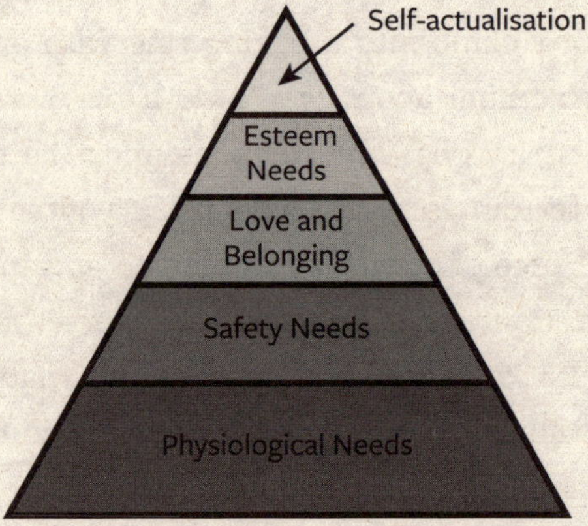

In the mid-twentieth century, a psychologist called Abraham Maslow wanted to find out how a person could live a life of maximum fulfilment. He asked successful and happy people what made them tick to see if there were any common denominators. He discovered the most contented were those who constantly looked to improve themselves, learn new skillsets and maximise their talents. They kept fluid, never got complacent, realised their potential and led a life of curiosity. This led Maslow to reflect that, 'If you plan on being anything less than you are capable of being, you will probably be unhappy all the days of your life.'

He famously wrote a theory called 'The Hierarchy of Needs'. The thrust of it is there are five kinds of need which dictate a human being's actions. If you imagine these needs as levels on a pyramid, the basic needs start at the bottom with physiological (food, water, warmth, rest); graduating to the next level, safety (security, shelter, institutions); then level 3, *love and belonging* (forming intimate relationships and having close friends); level 4, esteem (prestige and a sense of accomplishment in yourself) and finally, level 5, self-actualisation (achieving your potential and becoming who you want to be).

According to Maslow, you can only progress to the highest level once your first four basic need groups have been fulfilled. Think of it as a priority list and it really makes sense. For example, imagine a storyteller on an Arctic expedition. It's snowing, getting dark and despite the fact everyone is cold and hungry, he urges them to listen to him tell his story. Not surprisingly, it goes down like a lead balloon because all the other stuff is not squared away first. Nobody listens because they're all too busy shivering their balls off. Wouldn't it be better if the team were to put the tents up first, so they had shelters to retire to, somebody got the fire going and put the soup on, and everybody put on extra clothing to battle the cold, and only *then* sat down around the fire to hear the story?

The message is simple: unless we take care to prioritise

the **basic needs** first, the higher needs cannot be met. In another adventure context, you don't walk through a jungle to witness dawn rising over a Mayan temple (satisfying your higher need for self-development, which is all about seeing new things) without first taking care of basic physiological needs: getting sufficient rest, having the right clothing, enough food and water to protect us from exhaustion and overheating. The next level is our **safety needs**, like having a map so we know where we're going, and insurance in case there's an accident and we need to get helicoptered out of there.

The third level is **friendship** – who is going to come with us? A loved one or group of individuals whose company we enjoy and whose skillset contributes to the expedition. Level four is about **esteem and self-esteem**, both of which are equally important: do we have what it takes to make the walk? What's our opinion of ourselves? Do we have the confidence to do it? What of others' opinions? Do they think we have the minerals to go through with it? In order to get really good at something, we need the recognition of others to confirm our own beliefs in our self, otherwise we can become delusional.

The fifth and final level is **self-actualisation** – which we gain from the experience of visiting the Mayan temple. Self-fulfilment is achieved when we learn and enhance a new skill, be it cooking, surfing, filmmaking, bonsai growing, learning a new language, photography . . . whatever it may be. This fifth level is a standalone and can only flourish once the other levels are fully satisfied. Maslow calls these first four levels 'the deficiency needs' because if any one of them is not met the whole house of cards tumbles down temporarily until that singular deficient need is satisfied again. Even a great artist has to stop for food in between painting his masterpiece, just as a swimmer needs to hydrate between laps. You won't be able to reap much joy from sitting on that hill and watching the stars if you're too cold or your phone keeps pinging with messages from your bank telling you that you're overdrawn – immediately your mind will revert to safety and security needs, panicking about the financial wolf howling at your door.

In my opinion, it's not just about putting your boots on and wandering about aimlessly; you need to have a desired endpoint in mind before you go anywhere, and you prepare beforehand. And that's what the next section of this book is about: being prepared so you can really enjoy your moments of self-growth, wherever you're going, be it bivvying up on Snowdonia or on safari in the Kruger National Park.

SHELTER

Shelter, fire, water and food are the four pillars of wilderness survival. What kind of shelter you build will depend on how much time and energy you have, how long you think you'll be staying there, the level of daylight available and what raw materials you have in your immediate environment with which to make it.

Dos

Do build your shelter near the fringe of a wood so if someone passes, you can alert them to your presence – unless of course the idea is not to be found. Ensure there is plenty of fuel for your fire. If you're creating a temporary shelter, like a lean-to to evade freezing winds, make sure you are sheltered on the leeside (towards the wind), where you'll be protected from the wind, and that you have insulation on the ground to keep you warm. Only then you can start building a fire.

Don'ts

Don't build a shelter too close to a water source which draws insects, animals – among them predators. Also, there could be flash flooding and water trails will naturally lead to the body of water. Being too near babbling water impairs you hearing anyone nearby, be that rescuers or someone you need to take cover from.

Don't build a shelter at the bottom of a valley as, like a funnel, the wind will become more concentrated and stronger through this narrow area, and it's also where the cold and damp settles.

Also, avoid pitching your shelter on an exposed hillside as there will be nothing to break the force of the wind as it hits you. Avoid the shade of solitary trees in case of lightning. If you're building a shelter on the side of the hill, make sure you never sleep headfirst down the hill. I'm sure I didn't need to mention that!

And one rule of thumb: the bigger you build a shelter, the harder it is to heat and the less it will retain warmth. So, if you're surviving solo, make it just big enough for you to move around in.

Using what is naturally available

If Nature offers you a shortcut to building a shelter, take it. For example: large fallen trees and their upturned root system will provide an excellent hollow for shelter from poor weather. You can also dig a trench to deepen the hollow, adding branches to conceal its existence. Similarly, if you can spot a cave nearby that will keep you sufficiently dry and allow you to build a fire, use it. But only after scoping out it doesn't belong to a bear or mountain lion. Bones and scat are what you should keep an eye out for (see 'Wild Animal Attacks', particularly the sections on bears, pages 221–231). If you come across a half-eaten carcass with its intestines and offal neatly placed to one side, that is the work of a mountain lion. During the day, the animal will most likely be in the cave sleeping, emerging to hunt at dusk, retiring at dawn.

If you've crashed in an aircraft/truck/van and part of the vehicle is still temporarily habitable and will protect you from the elements, then utilise its solid coverage and protection. You'll need to fashion some kind of protective door to block out the rain, curious animals and the cold. Pile up loose branches, securing them with repurposed electric cable, rope or string, allowing for a small gap through which to enter and exit. Also, keep an eye out for crevices in rockfaces with sufficient depth that you can shrink back into them, beyond reach of the weather.

Even if you are in territory surrounded by predators, you've run out of food and are extremely tired, don't use your remaining energy to climb up a tall tree; big cats and black bears are much better than you are at scaling a tree. You are better off building a fire and gathering sufficient wood to keep it burning through the night. If you absolutely have to sleep in a tree, ensure you are roped to the bough to allow for sleep's sudden movements making you fall off.

Different kinds of shelters and how to build them

Lean-to shelter

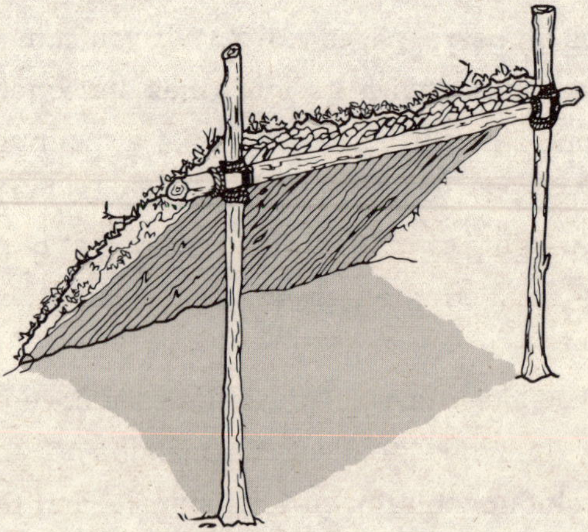

This is the quickest and easiest half-decent shelter to build, which will last you more than just one night. Place a strong stick or log around 10 feet long between the crotch (Y-shape where trunk and bough meet) of two trees to form your support cross bar. Alternatively, you can place one end of a long bough across the limb of a tree and its other end on the ground at an angle of 45 degrees to allow rain run-off, secured by two sticks forming a cross, tied together with your shoelaces.

Next, cover one side with branches, sticks, brush and fern to keep the snow or rain out. It's not very effective for insulation and not quite up to The Savoy yet, so if there is dry moss available try to roll back a section of it like you would garden turf and then unfold on the side of the shelter. You can also use moss to effectively cushion and insulate the floor of your shelter. If you are intending to build a fire within the shelter, ensure that your ceiling (the cross bar) is adequately high and you have a sufficient opening for the smoke to exit the space.

To regulate the size of sticks for your wall, you can snap them by wedging them in between two trees and using that as a pivot point. This saves you bruising your knee or gashing your hand, not to mention expenditure of precious energy.

A-frame

The A-frame shelter is exactly like the lean-to, other than it has two sides. You are basically leaning sticks and reinforcing them with branches, moss and leaves on both sides to create a tent-like shelter.

Cocoon shelter

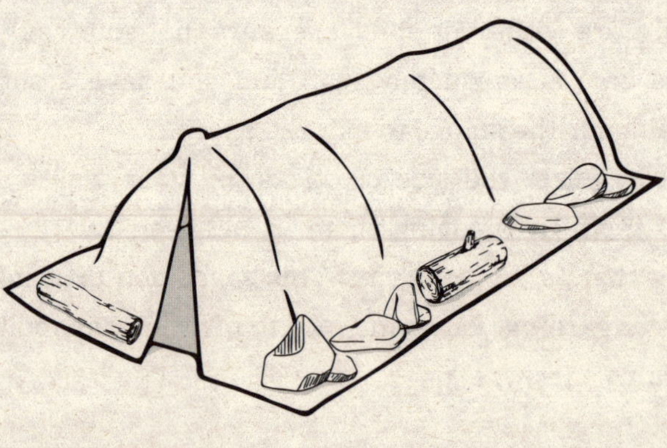

If you are extremely tired or don't have the light with which to build a more elaborate shelter, the cocoon is perfect for keeping warm and getting your head down for some much-needed kip. It's only an overnight option; you can build a much better one in the light. Look for a natural depression or hole in the ground in an area shaded by trees and use it as your base, packing the floor with moss and anything soft that will support your back. The deeper the sides of the hole the better as this will keep you shielded from the wind as much as possible.

You are essentially going to build a duvet of natural materials. Collect as many branches with foliage still attached as possible to use as the basic skeleton under which you will eventually sleep. On top of this skeleton place leaves, branches, ferns, moss – in fact, anything that will provide you a level of insulation from the cold. Given that this takes the best part of ten minutes to put together, don't expect too much from it; it might keep you warm but it's not going to keep you dry if the heavens open and it starts pissing down.

Sapling shelter

You can build a sapling shelter in just a few minutes. You'll need some rope and a tarp. If the environment permits and there are plenty of saplings, make a ribcage shape with five pairs of saplings, bending them and tying them up in the middle to form an arch. The resulting five arches form the linear skeleton of a shelter. Place a long piece of wood at their apex and through the middle. Throw a tarp over the top and keep it taut by putting large stones and logs along its base.

Tarp shelter

As the name suggests you'll need a tarpaulin or a poncho. Find two trees and tie each end of the tarp on one side to the trunk of the trees, then see if you can tie the other corners to anything on the ground. Alternatively, pack them with heavy stones and boulders to keep the tarp taut. Also, make sure you know where the wind is coming from. To do this, look at the movement of the branches or wet your finger and hold it up in the air to gauge which side of it feels the cold. The cold side obviously signals where the wind is coming from and will dictate on which side you erect your lean-to.

Tarp tent

This is just the same as the tarp shelter only in this case you hang an equal amount of the poncho/tarp on each of its sides and then secure it with rocks until it's taut. You will then need to barricade both open ends in order that nothing can get in. Use rocks and branches.

Snow trench

Dig a trench a little bit longer than yourself, at least a few feet deep. Using the snow that you've excavated, build up the sides of the trench and place sticks and branches across them to make your roof. Better still, shape the excavated snow into bricks of ice so they can lean against one another in the middle, providing you with a solid roof. In order to retain any heat, fill in cracks between the bricks with snow. Build the fire outside the entrance inside a ring of rocks to protect it from the wind.

Tepee

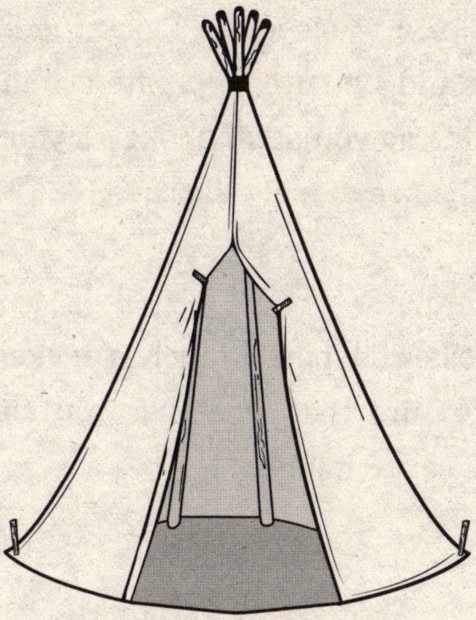

You'll need three equally long wooden poles of medium thickness to act as support legs. Lie them flat on the ground and lash them together at the top, interweaving the rope through them and repeating at least five times, so that when you lift them up vertically and separate the bottoms to form as wide a base as possible, they are still secured to each other at the top but now intersect. To create a chimney to allow for a fire inside the tepee, lash three pieces of wood close to the top of the tripod – one to each side of the cone in order to form a level on which you lean more poles against for added stability. Around this frame you can now place a tarpaulin. Make a slit in it to create an entrance and exit.

Snow cave

Select a thick drift of snow, checking that it is solid and firm. Dig a tunnel then hollow out a space, digging upward, creating a platform to sleep on. Block the entrance with your backpack and be sure to create a 6-inch breathing hole in the ceiling so you don't choke on your own carbon dioxide. Build the fire outside the cave.

Bedding

Dry leaves, moss and pine branches make an excellent mattress. Make sure that whatever you sleep on has a thickness of at least 8 inches.

WARMTH

If your core body temperature falls too dramatically this is when trouble really kicks in and your body starts working against you. At-29 Celsius in exposed air your body will freeze within five minutes. Since the early ages of man, when they used animal hide wrapped around their body, we have managed to battle the cold when outdoors by wearing plenty of loosely fitting layers which allow the body to breathe, wick away any sweat and retain heat. With the current hike in fuel bills many households are experiencing their first extended long-term encounter with the cold, only being able to occasionally turn on the central heating. Whether you are in a house or a makeshift shelter, insulation is key to trapping the cold. Old houses lose heat through drafts which get through warped window frames and gaps under doors. The quicker you can identify these heat haemorrhages and patch them up the better.

Getting naked in a sleeping bag if there are two of you is the best way to warm up someone suffering from cold by sharing your body heat. Heat is lost through the extremities – the hands, feet and head – so make sure you cover everything in order to retain your core temperature. Avoid staying in damp clothes if possible; dry them over the fire or in the sun. Wearing wet clothes will increase the speed with which you lose heat by 250 per cent.

How to build a fire

A crucial part to surviving in the wilderness is knowing how to build a fire so that we can stay warm and cook while out camping. For a fire to exist, we must remember the fire triangle: oxygen, fuel and heat.

For the **fuel**, you'll need tinder of some description. This is a fine, flammable material that catches alight easily, the most common of which is bark, moss, grass and leaves.

From the tinder, you can gradually build up your fire with larger dry twigs, sticks and branches.

Once you have your fuel ready, it's time for the **heat**. The most straightforward method is by using a lighter or matches, but a flint and steel fire starter kit is also a great option when these aren't available. Use them to create the spark needed for your tinder to catch light.

Finally, we're going to need to add some **oxygen** to the mix. More often than not, fuel and heat won't be enough, with a glowing ember rather than a roaring flame being the end result. The best way to properly get the fire started is to gather this ember and gently blow onto it. The addition of oxygen raises the temperature to the point where your tinder can now properly start to burn.

Creating a heat reflector

If you're in the wilderness it pays to create a heat reflector on the other side of the fire opposite you, so the heat is not lost but gathers in one place. To do this, you'll need four poles of equal length. Parallel with the shelter, hammer two poles into the earth close together with a small gap between them wide enough to stack poles horizontally so they are flush. You'll need to tie the parallel poles so they are secure before adding your cross beams.

FOOD

A balanced diet full of nutrients gives your body the fuel it needs to keep going, keep your brain active and your heart healthy. It also builds your muscles and strengthens your bones. There are three macronutrients for energy.

Carbohydrate: This is your prime source of energy. You can find carbohydrate in bread, pasta, fruit, vegetables, rice and sugar.

Protein: Builds muscle, helps repair your body's cells and is essential for a healthy immune system. You find it in meat, fish, chicken, beans, eggs, nuts, seeds, milk and tofu.

Fat: Gives you energy and provides a layer of insulation, as well as protecting your vital organs. It's also a source of fatty acids which help absorb vitamin A, vitamin D and vitamin E. Fat contains more calories than carbohydrates or protein, which the body can then turn into energy. In order to maintain body heat in extreme cold the body burns through calories much quicker than usual. You find fat in dairy products, red meat, nuts and avocados.

If you're out on an excursion, choose energy-rich foods that are easily grazable, lightweight, don't need to be kept cold and ideally don't have to be heated up. Great examples of these are:

- Trail mix of nuts, seeds and dried fruit, like sultanas and raisins
- Energy chews and gels
- Cereal bars
- Fresh fruit
- Tinned fish
- Cheese
- Nut butters
- Bagels

Foraging for food

The Earth is rich with animals and plants that can be eaten to sustain you in the wild. From delicious mushrooms to wild garlic and chickweed, everything you need to help you achieve your required amount of calories to survive can be found in Mother Nature's environment. For protein there are birds, small mammals, reptiles and insects, fish, nuts, eggs and fungi.

The following list will give you an idea of what to look for but you should get to know what is likely to be growing in the place you are exploring so you can confidently identify them in the field. The well-prepped survivor doesn't blindly eat the first juicy toadstool they see, but looks at its shape and colour to determine if it is poisonous or safe to eat.

Examples of plants, nuts and berries to avoid:

Honeysuckle
Lords and ladies
Poison ivy
Rhododendron
Hemlock
Horse nettle

- Foxglove
- Giant hogweed
- Bittersweet
- Moonseed
- Pokeberries
- Wild Cherry
- Virginia creeper
- Deadly nightshade
- Buckeye
- Laurel
- Dogwood
- Holly
- Wisteria

Examples of plants, nuts, berries and fruits you can eat:

- Crab apples
- Wild leeks
- Bilberries
- Rosehips
- Rowan
- Whitebeam
- Elderberries
- Hawthorn berries
- Japanese knotweed
- Common milkweed
- Hickory nuts
- Barberry
- Burdock roots
- Beach plums
- Catnip
- Stinging nettles
- Groundnut
- Pokeweed
- Sloe berries
- Wild cherries
- Plums
- Damsons
- Blackberries
- Wild strawberries
- Pine nuts
- Walnuts
- Mulberries
- Hazelnuts
- Pistachios

Examples of mushrooms to avoid:

Death cap
Jack-o'-lantern
False morels
Destroying angel
Panther cap
Fly agaric
Leaden entoloma

Examples of mushrooms you can eat:

Beefsteak
Honey fungus
Chanterelle
Field mushroom
Morels
Lion's mane
Giant puffball
Shaggy ink cap
Maitake
Oyster

Examples of edible fruits in the jungle:

Mango
Papaya
Fig
Coconut
Sugar cane
Durian
Banana
Yam
Grapefruit
Avocado
Pineapple
Orange

Examples of animals you should never eat in the wild:

Box turtle
Toad
Millipede
Centipede
Jellyfish
Pufferfish

Examples of animals you can cook and eat in the wild:

Caribou
Elk
Boar
Deer
Goat
Moose
Kangaroo
Rat
Bear
Salmon
Dingo
Alligator
Crocodile
Duck
Goose
Squirrel
Opossum
Seagull
Pigeon
Mouse
Rabbit

Examples of insects you can eat in the wild:

Bee and wasp larvae
Cicadas
Grubs
Ants
Termites
Worms
Snails
Slugs

WATER

Although our bodies are made up of around 65 per cent water, on the whole we struggle to drink enough water to filter the toxins from our bodies and keep them working well. Equally, we don't pay enough attention to where the water we drink has come from. I have my water distilled and add my own natural minerals.

Dehydration occurs when you're losing more fluid than you're taking in. An adult human can survive as long as three weeks without food but only three days without water. Ice produces twice as much water as snow when melted because it's compacted, so look out for blue ice for drinking as this is the cleanest. Keeping hydrated is crucial to surviving in icy temperatures because when you're hydrated your blood courses through your body to your extremities more easily. When you're dehydrated, your blood thickens and is harder for the heart to pump. This in turn affects the kidneys and draws fluid away from the brain, which affects cell function. When we're on the move we are constantly losing fluids through sweating, urinating and in the production of saliva. Signs of dehydration include headaches, muscle cramps, fever, fatigue, dark-coloured urine, disorientation and confusion, and an increased level of thirst. If your stool is black or blood-coated or you have diarrhoea things are getting serious.

Sourcing water

Water becomes even more crucial if you become lost and find your supplies are rapidly running thin. There are no corner shops in the wilderness for you to buy more, so what's the solution?

The best way of sourcing water, particularly in drier areas, is to observe the animals around you. Can you see frogs, mosquitos or flies? If so, you'll know water is close by. Ants are good to look out for as they're often heading towards reservoirs of water. Healthy-looking plants, particularly those with a greener colour, indicate that water is below the surface too.

How to purify water

Boiling water for a few minutes will kill the majority of bacteria that may cause you harm. Once cool, this will be safe for you to drink.

Another great way is by simply carrying iodine tablets. Drop one of these into the water to treat it, but don't be alarmed by the odd taste once the iodine has purified it.

NAVIGATION

You know where you want to go but if you don't know how to get there, then what's the point? Brushing up on your navigation skills is vital if you're going to survive when trouble strikes.

Maps

Maps are by far the best way to navigate. Make sure that you have a map case with a neck cord or pockets big enough for you to store them in so that they're easily accessible. Laminated maps are particularly useful if you find yourself in wet and windy conditions, too.

Use the contour lines of the map to help orientate you in the terrain: are you climbing uphill, downhill or on flat ground? Is the climb steep or gradual? Identifying landmarks and then locating them on a map will help you assess where you are.

Acquaint yourself with your map and study the different symbols in the key and what they mean before heading out into the wilderness. The Ordnance Survey offers great beginner's guides online: getoutside.ordnancesurvey.co.uk/guides/beginners-guides-map-reading/

Compass

The tiny magnet in your compass is controlled by the Earth's magnetic field. Your compass points to magnetic north, from which you can find true north. If you have an orienteering compass you can use this along with your map to take the bearing of your intended destination. It doesn't even have to be an orienteering compass – a small button compass is always handy to have on you in reserve.

If you don't have a map or compass, there are other alternatives. By day, you can mark your direction by studying the progress of the sun as it rises and heads to the west.

Navigating by stars

It makes no difference if you're on land or sea, plus it worked for the Vikings and will work for you too. First, pick out astar and, using a fixed point, mark its position in the sky. If the star rises from its original spot, you're facing east; if the star sinks, you're facing west; if the star moves to the left of its original position, you're facing north and finally, if the star moved to the right, you're

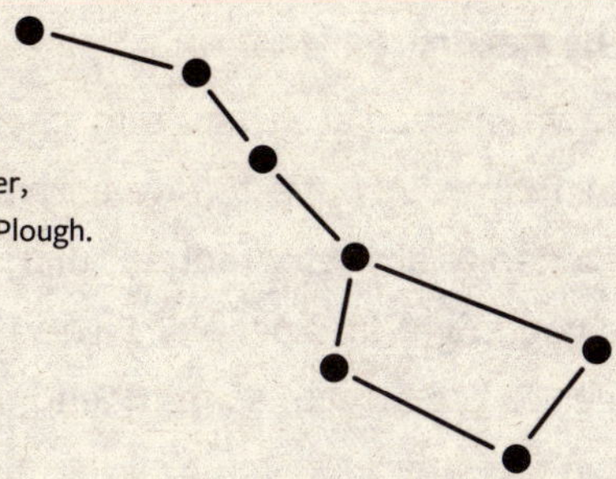

The Big Dipper, Saucepan or Plough.

facing south. As the Earth rotates in its orbit around the Sun, stars move across the sky. All except one, that constantly appears to be in the same place and that is Polaris, otherwise known as the North Star. It sits directly above the North Pole, so where you see it, that is your true north. The easiest way to find the North Star is by locating the Big Dipper, a constellation made up of seven stars. In the UK, we call it the Plough or the Saucepan. As it rotates clockwise around the North Star, its two lowest stars – the side of the saucepan away from the handle – point to the North Star, which is about five times further away than the distance between them.

In the southern hemisphere, there is no equivalent to the North Star, however, a constellation made up of five stars known as the Southern Cross telegraphs the position of the South Pole.

Determining north and south by a crescent moon is easy. Connecting the horns of a crescent by drawing a line from top of the crescent to the bottom gives you your north (from the top) and the south (the bottom). Extend that line down to the horizon for a more accurate bearing.

Navigating by nature

Depending on where you are there may be a stream nearby that you can follow. Always follow a river downhill. Its course may widen to a river which in turn may take you to a lake where you might find people. To find a water source, follow the bees or the insects as they tend to go about their business close to water.

HOW TO TIE KNOTS

These are the essential knots you should know, as well as what they are best used for.

Bowline

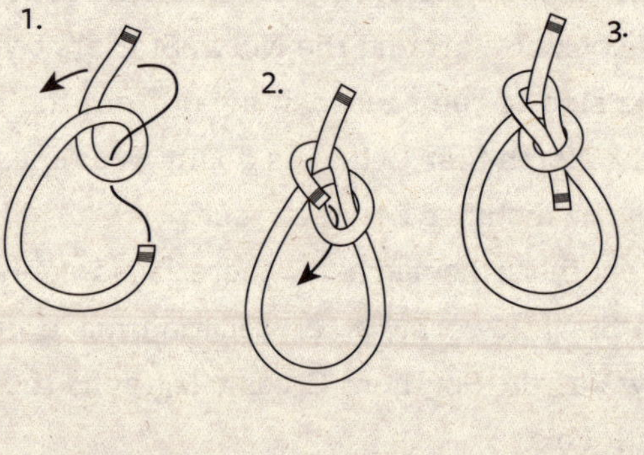

Step one: Make a loop in your rope with the working end over the top of your standing end. This loop is referred to as the 'rabbit's hole'.

Step two: Pass the working end of the rope up through the loop, so the rabbit comes up out of the hole.

Step three: Lead the rope around the back of the standing line so the rabbit goes around the tree.

Step four: Feed the working end back through the hole so the rabbit goes back into its hole.

Step five: Dress the knot (this is the process of making sure the knot is as efficient as possible) by pulling on the two strands of rope that go through the loop and the standing line, individually. Then pull all three individually to tighten your bowline.

The **bowline** is one of the most useful knots you can know, commonly used for forming a fixed loop at the end of a line.

Double figure 8

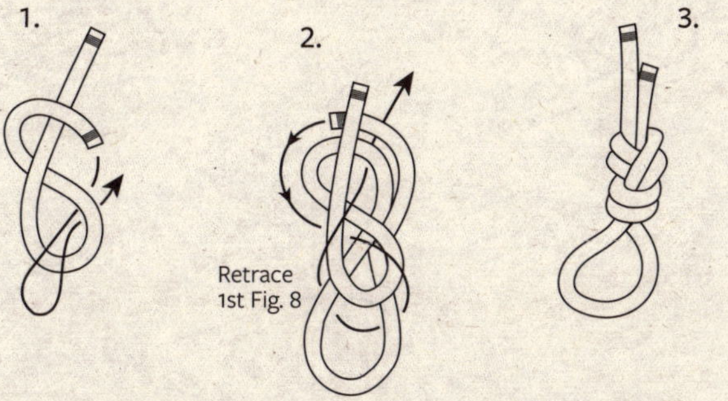

Step one: Lay out a bight (a U-shaped section) of rope. Each end of the loop must be several inches long to ensure you have enough rope to tie the knot.

Step two: Make a loop using the bight. Take the working end of your bight over the top of the standing end.

Step three: Take the working end of your rope around the back of the loop.

Step four: Feed the working end of your bight through the loop. At this point, your knot should look like a figure eight.

Step five: Tidy up your knot. You should aim to have a tail of rope that is 2–3 inches long to keep the knot secure. Feed rope through the knot to adjust the tail and the size of the loop if necessary.

The **double figure eight knot** is one of the most secure knots you can tie and is used for caving and climbing.

Clove hitch

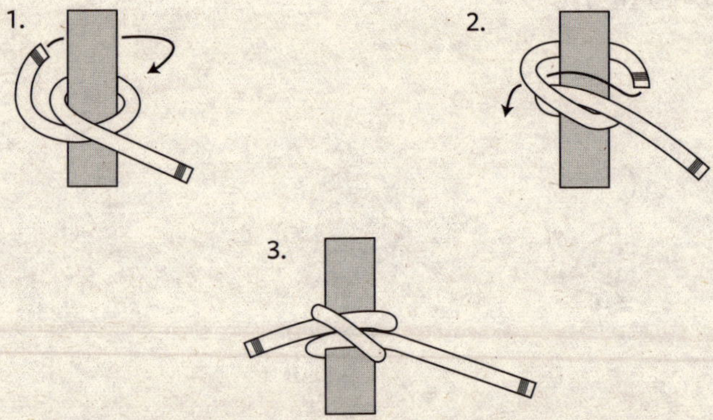

Step one: To create a clove hitch on a tree make a loop of long rope around the tree.

Step two: Make another loop and pass the working end of the rope under the second loop before tightening.

Step three: To tie this one over a post, create a loop in the free end of the rope and slide it over the post.

Step four: Now make another loop the same as the first and put the second loop over the post and tighten the hitch.

The clove hitch is a useful binding knot.

Square knot

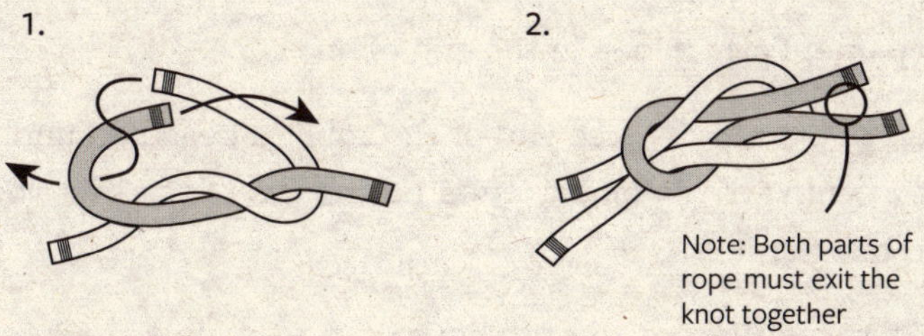

Step one: This knot is for joining two rope ends. Hold an end of the rope in each hand.

Step two: Pass the right hand over and under the rope in your left hand.

Step three: Pass the rope end now in your left hand over and under the one now in your right.

Step four: Tighten the knot by pulling both running ends at the same time.

The **square knot** is good for securing bandages and packages and joining two ropes together.

Double Sheet bend

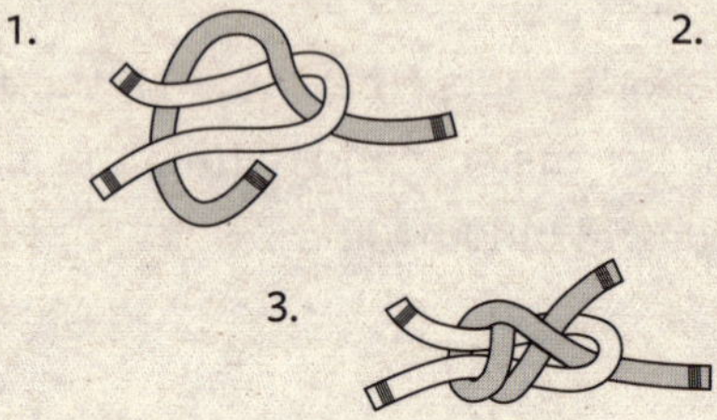

Step one: Form a loop in the end of one rope.

Step two: Pass the free end of the rope to be joined under the opening of the loop around both parts of the first row and back under itself.

Step three: Repeat the previous step to double the knot. Pull all four ends to tighten.

A **sheet bend** is useful for tying two ropes together.

Two half-hitches

Single Half-hitch

Two Half-hitches

Step one: Pass the running end of the rope around a post or through a grommet.

Step two: Bring the end over and around the standing part of the rope, then back through the loop that has formed. This makes a half-hitch.

Step three: Continue taking the end around the standing part to tie another half-hitch.

Step four: Pull the knot snug and slide it against the pole or grommet.

A **two half-hitches** is often used to tie up guy lines on a tent.

Taut-line hitch knot

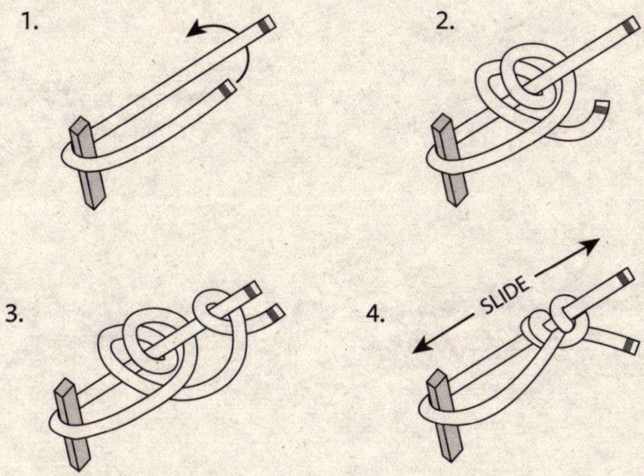

Step one: Pass the running end of the rope around the post or stake you want to secure it to.

Step two: Bring the end over and around the standing part, then back through the loop that has formed.

Step three: Go around the standing part inside the loop again.

Step four: Going in the same direction, take the end around the standing part outside the loop to tie another half-hitch.

Step five: Work any slack out of the knot, then slide the hitch to tighten or loosen the line.

A **taut-line hitch** is often used for staking out the guy lines on a tent.

Fisherman's knot

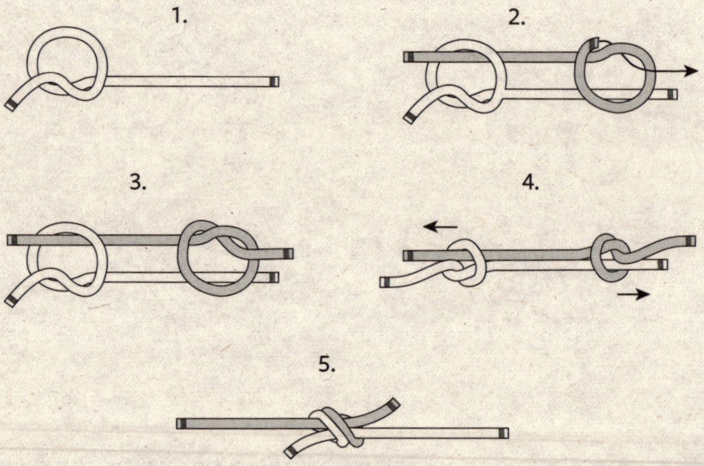

Step one: Tie a loose overhand knot with your first rope.

Step two: Thread the second rope through the loose knot of the first rope.

Step three: Tie a loose overhand knot at the other end of the second rope, looping the end of the first rope through.

Step four: Tighten the knot at either end.

Step five: Pull the standing part of each rope in opposite directions to bring the two knots together.

A **fisherman's knot** is used with fishing line.

Water knot

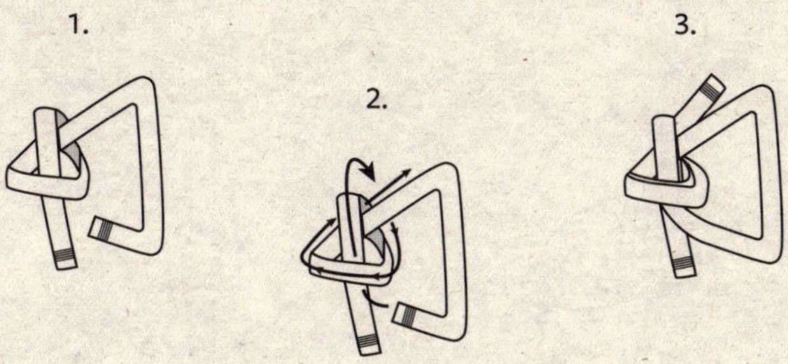

Step one: Start with a loose overhand knot in the end of one strap.

Step two: Pass the other strap in the opposite direction so it mirrors the root of the overhand knot on the first strap.

Step three: Take the ends of the two straps and pull the knot tight.

A **water knot** is often used for tying webbing.

Prusik knot

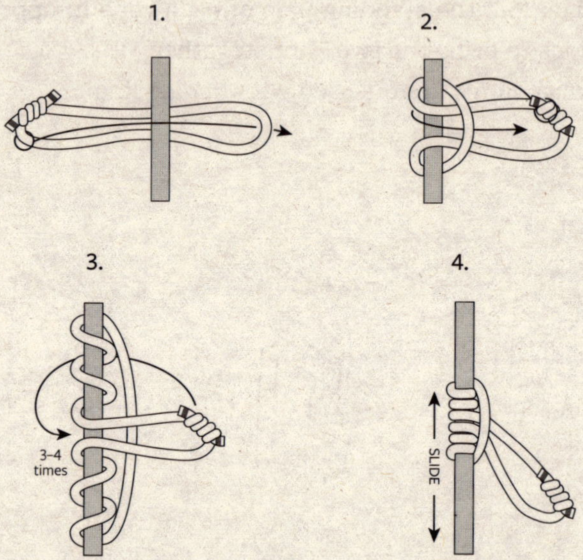

Step one: You need a short rope and a separate long rope. Wrap the loop around the long rope three times, making sure that each wrap lies flat against the long rope.

Step two: Pass the loop of short rope under itself and pull it tight.

Step three: As long as there is weight on the loop, pull the long rope.

A **prusik knot** creates a loop that can be used as an ascender or descender and is favoured by climbers, arborists and zipliners.

Rolling hitch

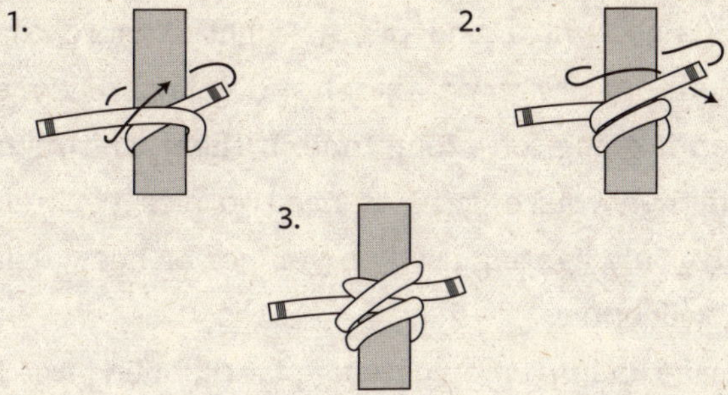

Step one: Wrap the free end of one rope around the main rope to create a half-hitch.

Step two: Make a second half-hitch and then wrap over the entire knot to finish with the final half-hitch to the other side from your starting place.

A **rolling hitch** adds a leg to an existing line and historically, it was used to hook more dogs to a sled mainline.

SENDING AN SOS SIGNAL

An SOS signal is an internationally recognised distressed call broadcasted in an emergency to seek help from others. We also use the term 'Mayday,' which comes from the French for 'help me', *m'aidez*. SOS calls always use the power of three, whether it's a smoke signal, a Morse code signal or flashes from a torch, or it's an aural signal, like a whistle or a gunshot. Make your way to high ground to telegraph light signals.

Using fire

Preparation is key. Build your fire up well in a clearing where flames will stand out at night. Ensure that you have plenty of dry wood, tinder and foliage ready, so you can keep it going for a long time. If there isn't much fuel to hand then you're going to need to pick your moment carefully, only lighting it when you see or hear a plane or rescue helicopter.

To make an impact on passing planes, build large letters 'SOS' out of wood and logs, then pour aircraft fuel or petrol over them and ignite. Ensure you have enough tinder to keep the fire going during the night.

Using smoke signals

Three fires are an internationally recognised distress signal. The light from a fire will only be visible at night but if it's not too windy, thick smoke can be seen from a distance during the day. Try to climb up to the highest altitude possible to set your fires as it increases the chances of your signal being spotted. You need to find a sufficiently large clearing away so the smoke has a chance to rise well above the forest canopy and the smoke columns can be seen. Make sure you have plenty of fuel to feed the fire.

Build the three fires in a triangle or in a straight line with about 30 metres (100 feet) between them. Add a layer of green leafy foliage to the flames as this will create a thick white smoke that can be seen from a distance. To control the plumes of smoke, wet a blanket and throw it over the fire.

Using a torch

Flash the light quickly three times, slowly three times and then quickly three more times. It's important to remember that the fast flashes should not exceed one second and the slow flash time should last longer than a second. This is SOS Morse code.

Using a mirror

This is the best method for trying to get the attention of an aircraft, ship, boat or other vehicle that's relatively far away. The first step is to aim the reflection of sunlight at the aeroplane or ship, then to reflect it three short times, three long times and another three short times – SOS. Heliography is the term for using the sun's light to transmit messages and dates back to ancient Greek times. Heliographic mirrors are inexpensive and well worth investing in as they have an eyehole to look through and a reflectorised screen that directs a beam of sunlight onto your desired target. Even if no rescuers are in sight, continue sweeping the horizon as mirror flashes can be seen for distances up to 20 miles.

If you don't have a mirror, you can use other objects such as a piece of broken bottle, tin foil or foil emergency blanket.

Using a flare

A distress flare is a pyrotechnic which creates an intense red flame. They shoot hundreds of metres up into the sky so are easily viewed from a plane or at sea. Obviously, there will be a limit as to how many flares you can carry in the event of emergency, so only fire a flare when you think there is a good chance someone will see it. The duration of the average flare is 40 seconds.

There are three types of distress flare: rocket parachute, multi-star and handheld – and they all are red. It is illegal in many countries to let off a distress flare other than in an emergency.

Using flags

If you have some brightly coloured material, use it to attract attention by attaching it to a long stick to make a flag. This will allow you to wave it more visibly and if you plant it in the ground while you are resting, it can still be seen.

Using Morse code

Tapping Morse code is a great way to signal for help in a confined space when others may be nearby as soundwaves travel effectively through solid objects. Try tapping on a window or on a pipe: remember, SOS is three times fast, then three times slow, then three more times fast. Or, in other words, dot-dot-dot-dash-dash-dash-dot-dot-dot.

Spelling out 'SOS'

Another visual way to attract attention from anyone above you is to use pebbles, stones and flotsam to create the letters SOS in an open space such as on a beach, making them as large as possible so they can be seen at altitude. If you've had a plane crash and are waiting to be spotted by a rescue helicopter or plane, salvage as many colourful and reflective objects and arrange them so a passing pilot can easily spot them on a flyover.

Body signals

Using body signals is an important way of trying to get attention and relaying your message, particularly as your first contact with the outside world is likely to be with a search aircraft. The body signals below are crucial to learn and have in your arsenal when all you have to send a message is your own body.

Using your iPhone

The iPhone has a built-in SOS feature. To use it, press and hold both the side button and one of the volume buttons simultaneously. You'll see an 'Emergency SOS' slider pop up on the screen. Drag the 'Emergency Call' slider to call emergency services. If you continue to hold down the side button and volume button instead of dragging the slider, a countdown begins and an alert sounds.

FIRST AID

The problem with us humans is that we get used to living in a predictable little bubble where most of the time it's extremely safe, and which leads us to get complacent and fail to plan for everyday emergencies. The problem is that when disaster strikes we're just not ready for it. For instance, in the event of your car breaking down in the middle of nowhere, do you have to hand the emergency telephone number of your breakdown service, or are you going to have to phone somebody to find it for you? You could Google it – if you have enough signal, of course. Do you keep emergency blankets in your car? Do you have a basic first aid kit ready in case a crisis hits when you're on the road?

A basic first aid kit should include the following:

- plasters in various sizes
- sterile gauze dressings

- eye dressings
- bandages
- disposable sterile gloves
- tweezers
- scissors
- cleansing wipes
- surgical tape
- digital thermometer
- skin rash cream
- aloe vera ointment for insect bites
- antiseptic cream
- antihistamine cream or tablets
- eye wash and eye bath
- paracetamol.

A friend of mine had a nasty fall from his motorbike and cut his femoral artery. He was rapidly bleeding out but fortunately, he had done some training in first aid and so he knew what to do in that situation, applying a tourniquet above the affected area to isolate the wound. If you were in a similar situation, would you know what to do? Imagine if it was a member of your family – you would want to take charge of the situation and be able to help them, right? We all know the answer to this and learning first aid is an easily achievable, brilliant life skill we can equip ourselves with, safe in the knowledge that if something happens, we'll know exactly what to do.

I remember a Virgin Airways flight attendant attended a weekend course my company, BreakPoint, held. Part of that course was first aid and a few months later, my wife Laura received an email from the flight attendant in which she said, 'Thank you, you saved my mum's life.' Apparently, her mother had fallen off the back of a boat into a lake and nearly lost her foot to the propeller. Thanks to her training, her daughter managed to stop the bleeding long enough to get her mum to the hospital and save her foot. She was prepared for the situation and instead of panicking she fell back on her training and knew exactly what to do.

In this section, we will look at how to deal with medical emergencies like anaphylactic shock, asthma attacks, diabetic emergency, bleeding, stroke and epileptic fits, as well as how to do CPR and apply a tourniquet.

Anaphylactic shock

Anaphylactic shock is a severe allergic reaction which threatens a person's ability to breathe. A person suffering from anaphylactic shock may experience swelling of their hands, feet, face, tongue and neck. They may also have an itchy rash. Their breathing will likely be affected, becoming laboured and slow. They may vomit or have diarrhoea. Anaphylactic shock can be caused by severe allergic reactions to pollen, insect stings and bites, and food such as nuts, shellfish, dairy products and eggs. The worst thing that can happen is the swelling of the airway, which means the person is unable to breathe.

People with known allergies usually carry something on them called an auto-injector, which contains medicine that will help ease the symptoms of anaphylactic shock. If they're unable to use this on themselves, you can do so for them by following the instructions on the product.

Asthma attack

If somebody suffers an asthma attack, the airways narrow, making it more difficult for them to breathe. Using an inhaler relaxes the muscles in the throat, allowing the airway to reopen. Somebody having an asthma attack will wheeze and cough and struggle to breathe. In extreme cases the person's lips may turn a grey-blue because there is insufficient oxygen in their body. If a person has become unresponsive, check that they're still breathing by tilting the head back, which releases the tongue and opens the airway. See if you can feel any breath coming from their lips onto your fingers.

Heart attack

Heart attacks occur when a blockage stops blood circulating to the heart muscle. The symptoms to look out for are a violent stabbing pain in the chest, breathlessness and sweating. A heart attack is the forerunner to a cardiac arrest, which is when the heart stops beating. A person experiencing cardiac arrest will become unconscious and collapse. Before this happens, give them some aspirin to chew slowly as it will help thin their blood. If it's too late then you will need to give chest compressions to keep the blood pumping around their body to their vital organs. To administer a chest compression, interlock your fingers with one hand on top of the other and using the heel of the hand push downwards firmly in the middle of the chest and release, then repeat. Keep doing this until the person regains consciousness.

Stroke

A stroke is sometimes referred to as a 'brain attack' as, similar to a heart attack, it happens when blood flow to part of the brain gets trapped or if a blood vessel in the brain bursts. When brain cells are starved of oxygen they die. Strokes are the biggest killer of men and a cause of long-term disability. There's also a worrying rise in young people: in the US, Sutter Health found that 10–15 per cent of strokes now affect those between 18 and 45 years of age.

If you suspect that you or someone else is experiencing a stroke, you need to act quickly and seek medical attention immediately. Every minute counts: the sooner a person receives treatment, the more likely they are to recover. The longer a stroke remains untreated, the greater the chance that stressed brain cells will die, leaving behind permanent brain damage.

The following acronym is really useful to help you remember the signs of a stroke:

Face – does one side of the face droop down?

Arms – does one arm drift downwards when both arms are raised?

Speech – is speech slurred?

Time – if you see any of these symptoms call the emergency services immediately.

Other signs of stroke include:

- sudden weakness or numbness on one side of the body
- loss of vision
- severe headache
- difficulty balancing, loss of coordination.

The risk of having a stroke can be lowered by various means:

- Paracetamol may help reduce your risk of stroke by preventing blood clots.
- High cholesterol and being overweight increase the risk of having a stroke. These can be managed by taking regular exercise and keeping your heart and blood vessels healthy.
- Quit smoking.
- Eat foods with less salt or sodium, which will lower your blood pressure, and stick to foods which are rich in fibre to manage your cholesterol.

- Speak to a doctor if your family has a history of strokes.

Recovery time after a stroke depends on the individual and the severity of the stroke. For some it may take weeks, for others, years, and a full recovery may not be achieved. Rehabilitation includes focusing on speech therapy, which helps the stroke victim to articulate more clearly; occupational therapy to help improve daily activities like dressing, bathing, drinking and writing; physical therapy using exercise to help with coordination, creating new neural pathways.

Epileptic fit

The obvious symptoms of an epileptic fit are when the person is collapsed on the ground, jerking and twisting about with foam around their mouth. The most helpful thing you can do is fold up a blanket or a jacket and put it underneath their head to protect it from the hard ground. Don't try to stop them from swallowing/biting their tongue as you risk yourself being injured. Also, don't try to restrain them. Let the seizure run its course and once finished, place them in the recovery position, lying on their side with the head tilted back, which ensures the airway is open for breathing.

Diabetic attack

Diabetics are in trouble when their blood sugar level becomes too low, either because they've over-exercised or haven't eaten. This can make them drowsy and confused and they will likely collapse. Give them sugar-rich drinks juice or isotonic sports drinks. Chocolate and sweets will also help raise their sugar levels.

Heatstroke

Heatstroke occurs when somebody loses too much fluid and stops sweating in hot conditions, or when they have has been exposed to the sun for too long and not drunk enough water. Physically, their body has become so hot that the brain's thermostat temporarily stops working. It doesn't have to be in a desert, it often happens to kids at the start of their holiday. Heatstroke requires immediate attention; if left untreated, it can quickly damage your brain, heart, kidneys and muscles. The longer the treatment is delayed, the higher the risk of serious complications or even death.

Signs of heatstroke to look for:

- sweating
- temperature rises to 40°C/100°F or over
- skin cool to the touch
- headache
- nausea

- dizziness
- confusion
- delirium
- slurred speech
- skin paler than usual
- vomiting
- rapid breath
- increased heart rate
- flushed skin from overheating.

What to do to bring the person's temperature down:

- Put them in a cool place
- Give them plenty of fluids – water or isotonic drinks
- Remove all of their clothing
- If they can stand, place them in a cool shower, spray them with a garden hose or put them in a tub of cool water.
- If the person can't stand, place them under a loose sheet and repeatedly pour cold water over them or constantly sponge them down with cold water
- Wrap ice in a cloth and place on their forehead, groin, neck and armpits
- Keep taking their temperature until it comes down.

If the person responds well to these curative measures and their temperature quickly returns to around 37°C, they no longer need a medical emergency team. However, to be on the safe side it's always better to call an ambulance in the *first* instance and use these measures above while waiting for expert help to arrive.

To prevent heatstroke:

- Keep topping up your fluids with regular sips of water; being hydrated helps your body maintain a normal temperature
- Wear a broad-brimmed hat if you're out walking under the sun
- Keep in the shade during the hottest part of the day
- Sunburn affects your body's ability to cool itself so wear sunscreen with a protection factor of at least 15, reapplying every couple of hours
- Wear loose-fitting, lightweight clothing which allows your body to cool
- Be aware of any medications you're taking that can affect your body's ability to stay hydrated or that may affect your heart
- It takes time for the body to adjust to hot weather, so gradually increase the time working or exercising in the heat until you are conditioned to it.

Burns

Burns are damage to the skin caused by heat. In the event of a burn, it's important to act quickly and worth remembering that the amount of pain you experience does not always correlate with how serious the burn is.

What to do:

- Cool the burn as quickly as you can with cool water, but never use ice as it can damage your skin
- Remove any clothing or jewellery from the burn area
- Loosely cover the affected area with clingfilm but don't wrap it. If you don't have clingfilm, use a clean dry dressing
- If possible, raise the affected area as this will reduce swelling
- Give the affected person paracetamol to relieve pain.

How to stop bleeding out

An adult has around 11 pints of blood circulating around their body. When somebody is bleeding profusely an urgent priority is of course to stop the blood escaping from their body. To do this, put pressure on the wound to allow the blood to coagulate for anything from five to 15 minutes. If it's a gaping wound, try to hold the edges together. If the afflicted feels cold and dizzy and the colour has gone from their face, they may be suffering from lack of blood, which could then lead to a heart attack. Have them lie down and lift their legs higher than their head so the blood flow to their heart and brain increases. Keep them warm with a blanket.

Applying pressure to a bleeding wound is the best way to encourage it to clot. In an emergency situation where medical help is not immediately available, these things may also help:

- Antiperspirant contains aluminium chloride which constricts blood vessels and helps a wound form a clot
- Some mouthwash contains alcohol. which acts as an astringent and helps the blood clot more quickly
- Distilled witch hazel is known to stop external bleeding
- Vaseline and many lip balms contain petroleum jelly, which can be used to stem bleeding. Wipe the wound free of blood first before you apply it
- Cold teabags contain tannins which cause the blood to clot; they also have antibacterial properties, potentially helping the wound to stay free of infection
- Applying ice wrapped in a clean dry cloth directly

on top of the wound constricts blood vessels, allowing a clot to form quickly

- By raising the affected area, you reduce the blood flow to it, which will help stop the bleeding.

Applying a tourniquet

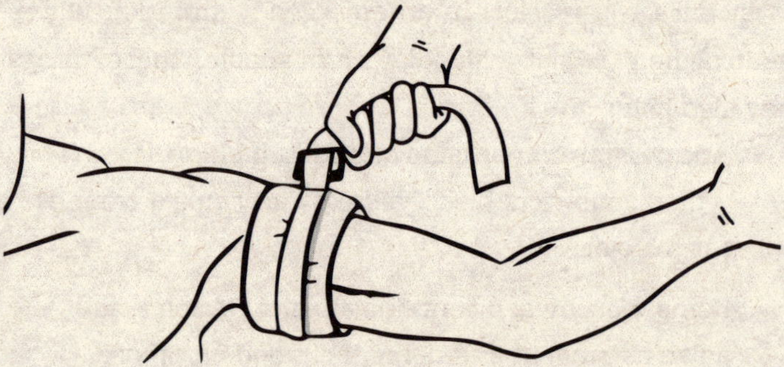

Applying a tourniquet above a wound (between the wound and the heart, in other words) can help stem excessive bleeding because putting pressure on blood vessels limits how much blood can get through to the wound. A tourniquet is needed if blood is spurting from a seriously deep cut or the injury has nicked an artery. Tourniquets can be applied to the arms and legs. If you're close to civilisation, then you need to call 999 but if you're out in the wild and someone suffers a serious cut and is losing blood, the first thing you should do is get the person to lie down with something soft under their head then follow these basic steps:

Step one: Find the source of the bleeding. If you're struggling to locate it then ask the person where they're feeling the most pain or if they feel a pulsating or numb sensation anywhere.

Step two: Remove any clothing that is covering the source of the bleeding. With a clean cloth, apply pressure to the key area from where the person is bleeding. You can quickly tell whether coagulation is happening or if they're still bleeding by how soaked the cloth you are using against the wound becomes. If after ten minutes a crust has not formed across the wound, apply the tourniquet.

Step three: Wrap the tourniquet around the injured limb 5–7 centimetres (2–3 inches) above the source of the bleeding. Ensure that the tourniquet is between the wound and the heart. If you don't have a medical tourniquet, you can make one by using a sock, tights, scarf, hand towel, resistance band, elastic bandage, or bandana. Avoid using a belt – people often try and tighten it in the same way as they would do around the waist, which will never be tight enough to stop arterial flow.

Step four: Next, tie a strong knot in the tourniquet, then improvise a windlass by placing a rodlike item in the tourniquet knot and twisting it clockwise to tighten its grip. Once it's tight enough, keep the windlass in place by twisting a rubber band or a hairband around it.

Things to avoid when applying a tourniquet:

- Don't place the tourniquet in an area which is not between the source of the bleeding and the heart
- Avoid placing the tourniquet on top of the source of the bleeding
- Don't place the tourniquet near to the joints – elbow, wrist, ankle, knee, etc.
- Don't apply the tourniquet to an area covered by thick clothing.

How to administer CPR (cardiopulmonary resuscitation)

If an adult casualty appears not to be breathing and seems unconscious when you try to wake them, they may have gone into cardiac arrest and you are going to need to administer CPR to get their heart going again. Turn them onto their back. With your elbows locked and your arms straight, lean over them and position the heel of one hand on the centre of their chest with the other on top of it, interlacing the fingers of both hands. Now compress their chest 5–6 centimetres (2–2.5 inches) in depth, 30 times, twice a second (if you know the Bee Gees' song 'Stayin' Alive' – and have a slightly dark sense of humour – sing this in your head to guide your tempo). After 30 compressions, give two moderate breaths mouth-to-mouth, first tilting their head back, lifting their chin and pinching their nose shut. Follow with another 30 compressions and two breaths and repeat until someone else takes over from you or the person becomes conscious again.

How to help someone who is choking

When someone's airway is blocked, inhibiting their ability to breathe, it's disturbing for the bystander and very frightening for the victim. The person's face will probably turn bright red, their eyes will water and they'll likely be panicking, gesticulating wildly and gagging. The next stage is a loss of consciousness as the brain is starved of oxygen. The longer that the person is out cold, the more irreparable damage to the brain is caused.

A common cause for choking is swallowing food too quickly without chewing it properly – foods that are the most common causes of choking are grapes, popcorn, hard-boiled sweets and chicken bones. It is also possible to choke on your own vomit if you are lying on your back. Kids may choke on foreign bodies like small bits of plastic toys they've been chewing on. Dysphagia is a condition where the affected person finds it hard to swallow because there is a delayed message from part of the brain to the jaw.

There are two types of choking – one when a person can breathe partially, the other when the airway is completely blocked. If they can still breathe, encourage them to cough up and spit out the impediment. Don't try to intervene by putting your fingers down their throat as they may bite you or you may push the object even deeper into their airway.

If the airway is blocked and they can't breathe, get them

to lean on your forearm while you stand behind them and slightly to the side. Clap them vigorously on the back five times between the shoulder blade with the heel of your hand. If that still doesn't shift it, then you need to try executing abdominal thrusts.

Note that this isn't suitable for children under a year old. If it's a toddler who is choking, lay them over your lap to administer the back claps. If this doesn't work, you will need to perform chest thrusts. Do this by laying the child on their back along your thigh. Locate the breastbone and put two fingers in the centre. Compress the chest to about a third of its depth.

The Heimlich manoeuvre

The Heimlich manoeuvre is a fancy term for administering abdominal thrusts to a person who is choking. First, stand behind them, place your arms around their waist, bending them forward. Make a fist with one hand and place it just above their belly button; with your other hand reach around their stomach and grab your fist, then pull sharply inwards and upwards five times.

Possible after-effects of severe choking:

- Choking is a terrifying experience to go through, whatever your age, and the aftermath may be one of anxiety towards food or even PTSD (post-traumatic stress disorder)
- Administering the Heimlich manoeuvre can cause

cracked ribs so only do so in the event of absolute emergency

- The lining of the throat may have been damaged by the object that was lodged in the airway
- The lungs may become infected due to food or liquids being inhaled, which can lead to aspiration pneumonia.

SLEEP

Sleep is one of the most important contributors to physical well-being. The right amount of it allows you to wake up feeling refreshed, balanced, energised and alert. The average person needs a minimum of eight hours sleep. While we sleep, our body and mind recharge. A lack of sleep can impair our immune system, reduce cognition and our ability to focus and think clearly. Worse still, a prolonged lack of sleep can lead to high blood pressure, diabetes, heart disease, depression and premature death.

Inbuilt in all of us is a body clock which regulates our sleep cycle, telling us when we're tired, and also when we're primed and ready for action. Its 24-hour cycle is known as the 'circadian rhythm'. There are four stages of sleep:

Stage one: Light sleep

Stage two: Deeper sleep – heart rate slows, breathing slows

Stage three: Heartbeat, brain activity, breathing and muscles all relax

Stage four: REM (rapid eye movement) occurs around 90 minutes after initially falling asleep. Dreaming typically occurs during REM sleep.

HYGIENE

Thorough personal hygiene is vital if you are to prevent the spread of possible disease and illnesses during a survival situation. Never neglect to clean your teeth twice a day; the alternative of an erupting abscess in the middle of a natural disaster does not bear thinking about. Washing your hands regularly with soap and water is also essential. If you have a family, you should also make a habit of this with your children to keep them healthy. Germs are easily transmitted from person to person, from unclean surfaces to our skin, or if you touch your eyes and nose or mouth, sneeze on your hand and then prepare food.

Hands should be washed for at least 20 seconds:

- before and after preparing food
- after eating
- if you are caring for someone who has diarrhoea or who is being sick
- after changing a nappy

- after going to the toilet
- after touching a pet
- before and after treating a wound.

In a disaster situation, the management of human waste can be disrupted by broken sewer pipes or no access to water. If water is no longer running from your taps and toilet flush, you'll have to improvise.

Using your own toilet: empty the water in the toilet, then use two plastic rubbish bags – one inside the other – to line the toilet. Put some sawdust or sand at the bottom of the bag and add some bleach. Remove and seal the bag after multiple uses each day. Make sure you wear gloves and boil wash the gloves in bleach afterwards. The bagged waste needs to be stored in an airtight container at least 60 metres (200 feet) from your home.

Creating a portable toilet: apply the same double-bag approach to a large bucket you can squat over. Or remove the seat part of a chair, replacing it with two short planks of wood with a gap in between to allow for defecation. Then set the chair frame directly over the bucket. Again, remember to put sawdust or sand at the bottom of the bucket bag and add some bleach.

In the absence of water ensure you have plenty of handwipes or hand sanitiser liquid for basic hygiene. Check the latter has at least 60 per cent alcohol in its contents. It's estimated that 700,000 deaths occur annually around the world because of a lack of access to handwashing facilities.

Here's a list of the basic toiletries and equipment you should have in your kit:

- Toilet paper, at least two weeks' worth
- Wet wipes
- Towels
- Anti-bacterial handwash
- Bleach
- Toothpaste
- Toothbrush
- Shampoo
- Dental floss
- Nail clippers
- Protective rubber gloves
- Soap
- Strong, sealable bin bags
- Sand, kitty litter or sawdust
- Tampons, sanitary pads.

BREATHING

When your heart beats quicker because you're panicking, your metabolism speeds up too and before you know it, you're more hungry than you were. Taking deep breaths to regulate any rising panic is an important first step –

getting stressed will achieve nothing but a cloudy brain and in this situation, you need to gather your wits. You need to re-orientate yourself. The Special Forces operator has a saying to help keep them calm in such a situation when panic starts to settle in:

BREATHE: Relax and focus on your breathing

RECALIBRATE: Assess the situation to one or two things which you are in control of, like the ability to slow your breathing

DELIVER: Take appropriate action as a result of your newfound clarity of thought.

Box breathing

One way to relax and focus on your breathing is to try something called 'box breathing'. Find some kind of seat and place your hands on your lap with your palms facing upwards. Try to blank out any of the noises that surround you. Tune it all out. Go to step one.

Step one: Exhale slowly through your mouth, getting rid of all your breath.

Step two: Inhale through your nose while counting very slowly in your mind to four. You should breathe to the very base of your back and feel your shoulders rise with all the air in your lungs.

Step three: Hold that breath for another count of four.

Step four: Exhale slowly through your mouth to the count of four, focusing on the air leaving your lungs and exiting your lips.

Now repeat the process from step two. In addition, it can increase the effect if you exhale for slightly longer than you inhale, so for instance increase the exhale to the count of six.

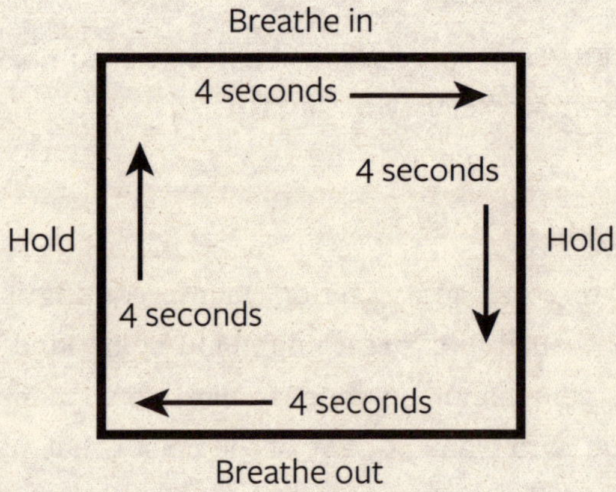

When focusing on deep breathing, we can calm our automatic nervous system, which regulates our body temperature, lowers blood pressure and gradually calms us down. For those of you who'd like the science of what's happening: holding your breath allows CO_2 to build up in your blood, which stimulates the vagus nerve when you exhale, to trigger your parasympathetic system, which in turn produces a calm, relaxed feeling in the mind and body.

PLANNING AND PREPARATION

So, you've now equipped yourself with the essential skills and knowledge to survive out in the wilderness, along with understanding what kind of tools you'll need. But how do you sufficiently prepare for major life upheaval? You can never be too prepped. Obviously, your level of prep depends on where you are and what you're facing. For example, if you live in an area where it snows heavily, you'll know to get things in place for winter, so that should a blizzard or ice storm make it too dangerous to go outside, you'll have at least two weeks' worth of non-perishable food and water supplies on hand. If you have an ongoing illness that requires regular medication, ensure you always have a back-up supply stashed away. And you'll need food for your pets, if you have them, and plenty of nappies for your baby. And if you're imminently expecting a new addition to your family and you find yourself housebound then you will need to be able to access advice on home-birthing. Having a solar-powered heater in case the grid goes down is equally vital. Make sure you have a generator, access to fresh water, plenty of torches and spare batteries, wood for the fire . . . books or games to keep your kids amused and things to do that will stop you all going stir-crazy. This is just a working example of preparing for one situation and much of it is simply common sense.

Prepping a 'get home' bag

It's quite likely you'll be away from your home and at work when disaster strikes. **A 'get home' bag** should be stored somewhere accessible, like in your car or under your desk, and should include the following:

- knife
- first aid kit
- ID
- credit card
- money in small denominations
- water
- water purifying tablets
- energy bars
- change of clothes
- comfortable footwear
- emergency whistle
- torch and spare batteries
- map of the local area
- wind-up radio
- list of important numbers
- fully charged portable charger for your phone and any other electronic devices.

If you drive to work, always make sure that you have enough fuel to get you home, with a jerry can of fuel in the boot in case you run out too.

Bugging-in

Bugging-in is when you make the decision to stay at home and ride out disasters and dangers happening outside. Remember the movie *Home Alone* with that resourceful little boy called Kevin, who accidentally got left behind when his family went on holiday to Paris, and he then took on two bungling burglars? That's the kind of thinking you need to employ when it comes to tricking the criminal mind.

In the event of opportunistic criminals, it's always good to be able to give the impression that you're in when you're out. I'm not suggesting that you go quite so far as Kevin did, laying hammer traps and creating life-size cutouts on a pulley system that you operate by pulling the strings, but there are some brilliant apps available with which you can remotely control the lighting, sound systems and radios in your home from your mobile phone. Remember that most burglars operate between 10am and 3pm when most people are out. If a criminal sees that the lights are on in the morning, they'll take this as more of an encouragement than a deterrent to come and take a closer look at your house, as most people don't need the lights on if it's fully light outside.

As a basic anti-burglar requirement, you should have

visible CCTV placed around the outside of your property. Motion sensor lights should be well located so anyone entering your home's perimeter will be immediately visible. Your alarm should be high-quality, loud and rapid to deter intruders. Signage indicating that CCTV and alarms are in use around the property and also 'Beware of the Dog' signs even if you don't have any of the above are still a deterrent that's better than nothing. Place stout locks on every downstairs window.

What if it's a horde of desperately hungry people trying to get in? You'll need more than motion sensor lights and a phone app to keep them at bay. Your home is your castle and you must make it as self-sufficient and safe as possible against whatever is happening outside of it, whether it's extreme weather or social unrest that comes battering at your door. Your house is familiar to you, you know it's layout and escape routes, you have plenty of storage space and, most importantly, it's home – of course you'll want to stay here as long as possible in the event of a disaster.

There are ways you can fortress your house without it being obvious; getting bulletproof glass installed is an option. Painted steel shutters can look attractive on windows and be a useful layer of defence when closed and locked in place. And a steel front and back door would secure your points of entry. A steel-walled 'safe room' you can lock yourself in in case of your house being overrun by strangers is a good last resort option, but only if you have a panic button that connects directly with a dedicated security team or the local police station who will come and rescue you if it's pushed. In a social unrest situation, you must ask yourself if the police force would be too overstretched to be able to respond to you. The safe room should be comfortable and also well-stocked with plenty of water and food.

Bugging-out

When it's no longer safe to stay in your house and bug-in, that's when you will need to leave and take your family to a specified bug-out location. Make sure your emergency vehicle is close to the house. Bugging-out is a last resort you really don't want to have to take. A bug-out shelter is not something that can be built over a weekend, it requires a sizeable investment over time and is a big undertaking. Remember, this will be your second home for an undetermined amount of time.

A lot of people get romantic ideas about bugging-out in the most remote places possible, like a desert island or a distant forest where no one will find them. But before you decide to build a bug-out shelter, you need to think how long it will take you to get there and what areas will you have to go through to reach it, which may put you and your family in jeopardy. It doesn't have to be an underground bunker, nor does it have to be a Swiss Family Robinson-style treehouse a hundred feet up a Sequoia tree; it might just be a relative's home in a different area.

Your bug-out location depends on a number of things, such as how agile you are as a family; for instance, does someone in your family have special needs that require specialised technology to aid their movement? Could you transport them by foot across rugged terrain? Would you be in danger yourself if you tried to do so? Does your bug-out plan include taking your parents, and if they're very elderly, how are they going to manage? Just by starting to consider these basic logical difficulties helps you to choose a location which is realistic and achievable.

A bug-out location should be determined by what the most probable danger will be. If it's nuclear war that you fear, your shelter needs to be a safe distance from the nearest city, whereas if it's societal breakdown that you believe may happen, it not only needs to be a fair distance from the city but as remote as you can possibly get; both radiation and rabidly desperate humans in pursuit of food are both capable of covering long distances!

Bug-out bag

A bug-out bag contains all the basic items you will need to last you for three days in the event of having to evacuate in an emergency. It should be stored somewhere accessible so you can grab it and get out of your house as quickly as possible. Every member of your family should have their own BOB (bug-out bag). It's probably easier if they're all kept in the same place then you don't lose valuable time. A bug-out bag should contain at the very least:

- knife
- first aid kit
- 1–2 litres water
- mobile phone with GPS
- satellite phone
- water filter
- non-perishable food, glucose energy tablets, energy bars
- any prescription meds and an official letter from your doctor as to what you take them for
- change of clothes, underwear
- cash
- trail shoes with ankle support
- compass
- SOS flares
- waterproof clothing
- personal hygiene items, such as wet wipes, toilet paper, tampons, sanitary pads
- emergency whistle
- duct tape
- ID and photocopies of important documents in a sealed waterproof bag
- flashlight and spare batteries

- toiletries
- bin bags
- paper and pens
- cordage – rope or paracord – suggested length 5m, kept on a spool for easy storage
- map of the local area
- wind-up radio
- list of important numbers
- portable shelter, like a poncho, bivvie or tent
- battery charger for your phone
- space blanket
- pet food

Cache

This is a hidden supply of food and provisions which will be kept somewhere en route to your bug-out location. Everyone in your family should know exactly where it is in case you get separated, although to be on the safe side, you should mentally note down the details of the visual position of where your cache of emergency supplies is hidden, just like Andy Dufresne did to his pal Red in *The Shawshank Redemption* when he told him to look for a hay field with a long rock wall and an oak tree. Though while it's great to have visual clues, in an emergency you don't want to be scrabbling about like a pirate searching for where X marks the spot. You need to know exactly where it is. And what if it's been snowing and your visual clues are blanketed? So make sure the exact position of your cache is also located with GPS coordinates and on a cache map which you share with all the family. Ideally, you should have three points to take a bearing from, such as a tree or rock or any permanent structure, including a number of paces to the cache. All three lines will then cross at the same point, which will indicate where the cache is. Include the depth of the cache to avoid you digging for days when it's a metre to the left and only 50 centimetres down. Another good bit of kit to take is a probe or long tent peg to penetrate the ground and establish location before digging.

Your cache should contain emergency food and water supplies and another first aid kit, as well as blankets, a change of clothes for all the family and ammunition if you're carrying a firearm. It should be kept in an airtight, waterproof bag and buried in a hole under the ground. Ensure that you scatter leaves or greenery on the surface above where you buried your emergency bag, so it looks natural and undisturbed.

PART THREE:

CLIMATE AND TERRAIN

EXTREME COLD

Many of the suggestions in this section are based on my own experience as a mountain climber and expertise in surviving the cold learnt during my arctic warfare training in the Special Forces. But there's a great many tips here that spring from having a bit of common sense and forward thinking, which we are all capable of.

According to *National Geographic*, global warming can cause harsh winter weather because a warmer atmosphere can hold more moisture, which causes an increase in precipitation, hence more snowfall when temperatures are below freezing. We need to get used to arming ourselves with the right protection to ensure we come through unscathed – be it wearing enough layers, getting tyre chains to keep our cars on the road, carrying emergency foodstuffs with us if we're driving in snow, as well as spare fuel to keep our vehicle's heater going if we get stranded.

When going anywhere in the cold we should have the proper gear as well as emergency supplies. A basic kit might consist of something like this:

- snowshoes
- space blanket
- water

- snacks
- energy bars
- compass
- sat nav device
- plenty of layers of clothing
- first aid kit.

Ollie Experience: Arctic training in Norway

During my time in the Special Forces, while I spent a lot of time on the water, most of it was spent beneath it, freezing my nuts off. In Norway, during Arctic training, we would climb through a hole in the ice at night and practise underwater navigational skills with a compass. Despite having a neoprene wetsuit on you're still freezing, so it was vital that you kept moving to boost your circulation. Another drill involved climbing out of the ice and then removing your wet clothes and rolling in the snow so that it absorbed the freezing moisture from your body. Just as in the water, you can't stop moving for even a second, to keep your blood flowing through your body to avoid hypothermia.

While filming the *SAS: Who Dares Wins* series in Chile, we recreated some of the Special Forces exercises around adapting to the cold. Wearing clothing rather than a neoprene wetsuit, I had to demonstrate remaining calm while climbing through a small ice hole and standing still in freezing cold water. And to lead by example, which meant keeping a brave face on for the recruits who were watching my every move. It had been a long time since I'd last done this and spent time conditioning my body to extreme cold, so in this instance it was mostly a case of mind over matter – not helped by the fact that my head was so freezing I had the worst case of 'ice cream headache' imaginable!

Next, I had to submerge myself in the cold water and swim ten metres underwater beneath the ice and then pop out of another hole at the other side, then swim another ten metres to ascend from yet another hole. All in a day's work.

If you are going to be part of an expedition and will be crossing ice then it makes sense to start training your body and breathing for the intense eventuality that you fall through, god forbid it happens. Once your body has experienced, reacted to it and survived you'll have better muscle memory if the real thing happens; you'll be calmer and more in control of your breath.

Cold water showers are all the rage at the moment, as are ice baths. What they do is put your body under stress as it attempts to adapt to the sharp drop in temperature. And while shivering your nuts off might seem a world away from the kind of stress you experience at work or in your home life, as far as your body is concerned, stress is stress and will elicit the same chemical reaction, no matter what context that stress may be wrapped in. Cold water stress tolerance when practised regularly can massively help you feel more resilient to dealing with general life stress.

To adapt to the cold, start off with few layers so you feel cold, then gradually add just enough layers. Living in an overheated cocoon is doing nothing for our health and resilience to the cold. These practices, along with the above kit, are essential preparations for surviving the extreme cold.

Case Study: 'Touching the void'

In 1985, Joe Simpson and Simon Yates successfully summitted the Siula Grande, a 6,344-metre mountain in the Peruvian Andes. Having taken the route through the virginal west face, they began their descent on the north ridge, a lethal cluster of fragile cornices. Yates was the first one to take a fall as he walked up to the tip of a cornice in a whiteout. The cornice collapsed and suddenly he was dangling from the end of a taut rope with a 1,300-metre drop beneath him.

That night, they dug a snow hole and ate the last of their food, using the last gas canister for their stove to boil snow they could drink. The next day, the climbers were in a desperate rush to get down as quickly as possible and, while moving blindly through a whiteout, Simpson fell down an ice cliff and landed badly on his right leg, the tibia thrusting through his knee joint. Plagued by terrible weather they needed to get down as quick as possible but Simpson was unable to put any pressure on his leg.

The only way Simon Yates could get him down the remaining 900 metres to the glacier was by tying two ropes together and using a belay plate to gradually allow Simpson to descend. Yates dug himself a hollowed-out bucket seat in the snow from which he could have a little more traction while holding the rope. It was agonisingly slow work but they made a good deal of progress. Suddenly, the mountain's face turned vertical and Simpson found himself dangling free of the rockface with all his weight putting pressure on the rope and Yates, who was trying to hold him. It was only a matter of time before Yates would be pulled out of his home-made cavity and slide down the cliff to follow his colleague.

Yates clung on for 90 minutes, wondering what to do, and then made the decision to cut the rope – it was either do or die. Yates's instinct to survive was stronger than his loyalty to his friend; he wanted to see another sunrise. As he cut the rope it was still dark as Simpson fell some 200 feet, smashing through the roof of a crevasse and continuing to fall until he landed on an ice bridge. When he pulled the rope above him and it landed in his lap, he could see that Yates had cut the rope but bore him no bitterness.

Simpson's only way to go was down and he lowered himself into the darkness of an unknown abyss with his faith and weight resting on a solitary ice screw. Things finally began to look up for him when he lowered himself onto a solid surface with just a few feet of rope left to play out. In the far distance, a spear of light shone through an aperture in the ice cave – his exit route out onto the glacier, he hoped. It would be a hard and dangerously slippery journey to get to that light even for an able-bodied climber, but Simpson, not to be beaten, and furious with himself for allowing the situation to have got to this, set himself micro targets along the way, thereby chopping up a near-impossible task into digestible chunks of 20-minute targets.

When he finally reached the opening of the cave his triumph was short-lived; stretching out before him was a vast icescape of hidden crevasses. And then he spotted Yates's footfalls in the snow and started the long shuffle on his behind in pursuit of them. For three days he fought delirium, incredible pain and the paranoid anxiety that his climbing buddy and another guy called Richard, who had stayed at base camp to watch over their things, would have gone by now. He sucked on ice to hydrate, continued setting 20-minute micro challenges and eventually, on the third night, he reached their camp.

Since this nightmare adventure the two are no longer friends, but Simpson maintains he would have made the same decision as Yates to cut the rope; in fact, he even claims he would have cut the rope and sent himself to the hell that awaited him in the crevasse, had he possessed a knife.

Hypothermia

Hypothermia happens when you're exposed to cold, wet or windy conditions, or when you're in direct contact with something very cold. In any of these situations, heat is conducted away from your body and to regulate your core temperature at a safe level the body expends energy. Once your stored levels of energy are spent and your body begins to lose more heat than it can generate, this is when hypothermia sets in.

The signs of hypothermia

Mild – Following severe shaking, which is your body's attempt to warm itself up through movement, you will experience a gradual loss of motor control in your hands and feet, making it harder to move about. A slowing down of the mind, disorientation and tiredness will follow. Turning pale, shivering, falling over and an excessive need to pee are also symptoms.

Moderate – Abnormal heart rhythm, slurred speech, headache, bluish-hued skin, low blood pressure, slow reflexes, dilated pupils. At this point, breathing slows down and mental cognition becomes shaky.

Serious – Fluid in your lungs, coma, not going to the toilet to pee, low blood pressure, cardiac arrest.

How to avoid hypothermia

In extreme cold avoid doing exertion that will cause you to sweat profusely – wet clothes combined with freezing temperatures will rob you of body heat. Wool or silk inner layers retain body heat well and water-repellent outer jackets and trousers are best for fortifying yourself against chill winds. Cover your face and ears with a scarf or balaclava; wear a warm hat to keep the heat from radiating from your head.

How to treat hypothermia

If you're taking care of someone else with hypothermia, first up, you need to get their wet clothing off, gently replacing it with dry clothes. Don't make any jerky movements and be careful not to move them too roughly (if you have a knife available, cut the wet clothes off as quickly as possible). The temptation might be to rub them vigorously to warm them up but if someone is in a hyperthermic state too much movement can cause cardiac arrest, as can warming them up too quickly, so *gradually* apply towels and blankets - anything dry - which will warm the body up again.

The body temperature will continue to drop if they are lying on a cold icy surface. If you've got a first aid foil blanket then place this on the ground next to the person and very gently roll them into the recovery position (see also page 74) on the blanket, tucking it around them. Then gradually place blankets and coats to insulate the warmth created. If you have pocket warmers or hot packs then the places you need to apply them are the chest, neck and groin. Make sure they are covered from the neck down to their toes. Try and get them to drink a little water.

Ollie Experience: Pit stop

For the 'escape and evasion' stage of Special Forces selection you are given First World War fatigues made of horsehair, a T-shirt, a heavy great coat and boots without socks. It was freezing up in the Brecon mountains where we were doing the exercises and we managed to get to a barn and take off our shoes. All I can say is it's a good job the farmer didn't open the barn door and look in at that moment, because in order to warm up our cold-crucified trotters, it was necessary to split into pairs and put our feet in each other's armpits. I'm glad to report it worked!

Frostbite

Diabetics, smokers, children and the elderly are more prone to developing frostbite, as are those who are dehydrated, improperly dressed for freezing weather and those who have been drinking alcohol. Over-exposure of naked skin to freezing temperatures can quickly turn to frostbite. It affects the extremities of fingers, ears, toes, nose, feet and cheeks. Initially, the affected area will feel numb or tingly. There are three stages of severity.

Stage one: First degree frostbite, known as 'frostnip', sees the skin turning pale white or blue, and swelling and blistering an angry red.

Stage two: Surface frostbite occurs when the water in your skin turns to ice crystals. Tingles turn to sharp stinging pain; the affected area turns red, purple and blue, blistering and peeling. The skin may also swell up with pockets of fluid.

Stage three: Severe frostbite attacks the layers of subcutaneous tissue beneath the skin. As cells die, skin turns black and becomes numb. A hard carapace forms upon it like a black mummified crust and may involve the limb, finger or affected area needing to be amputated to avoid gangrene.

How to avoid frostbite

Frostbite can occur within 30 minutes in temperatures below freezing and the numbness and pins and needles that first set in can make you clumsy and stiff. There's a greater chance of it developing when there's a high wind chill factor. If you can catch it at the frostnip stage and rewarm the area, you should be fine. Unfortunately, once you've had frostbite, it's easier to get it a second time. It can also settle as arthritis in the joints, months and years later. One way to tell if your frostbite is serious is to examine your blisters – if they are clear then the damage is likely temporary but if they are full of blood, the damage will be long-term.

In freezing temperatures or when the wind chill is high, avoid being outside any longer than ten minutes. Layer your clothing, ensuring it's loose enough not to trap your circulation. Wear two pairs of socks, thermal vests, a thick hat which covers your ears and a balaclava, scarf or snood over your entire face. Mittens are better than gloves as your fingers together create more heat and therefore better circulation.

How to treat frostbite

You have very little time to stop the spread of frostbite once it has set in. At stage one frostnip, get inside a warm shelter or vehicle, removing all material and treat the skin with lukewarm but *never* hot water. Then dry and wrap in sterile bandages, ensuring affected toes or fingers are separately wrapped to avoid painful rubbing. If you're lucky you will be able to get to a clinic while it is still at stage one and the worst you can expect is chilblains (small red bumps). Don't go out into the cold weather again the same day, even if you have warmed up. If this is not possible and you're way out in the boonies, warm your skin in water no warmer than 40.5°C until it softens. Don't walk on frostbitten feet and elevate the affected area slightly. Take antibiotics, which you should always have with you as an emergency cover, anti-inflammatories and painkillers, and make sure you constantly hydrate.

Sir Ranulph Fiennes, former SAS soldier and the world's greatest living explorer, had to turn back from his solo attempt to walk unsupported to the North Pole having developed severe frostbite of the fingers. Back in the UK, he was in such pain he took himself into his workshop and removed the offending digits with a circular saw – so take note!

Snow

The challenges severe snow brings with it, whether you're caught in a whiteout in Banff or walking the icy drifts of the Arctic, mean you need to be able to understand the snowy landscape and the lethal dangers it blankets beneath it, like crevasses. But let's not forget, many cold weather accidents also occur close to home. Because of the proximity to what we regard as safe and familiar, complacency overrides common sense and we think we can busk it; we won't get caught in a snowdrift or slide off the road.

It's worth remembering that a freshly fallen blanket of snow can effect a profound change on what was formerly well-known terrain. You may be very familiar with the landscape during the summer, autumn or spring, but when covered in snow, it's much easier to miss key waypoints that usually point us in the right direction. Assess the risk before you go anywhere, even if it's a case of walking up a familiar hill. Remember that what was a layer of soft powder in the morning, come late afternoon with the falling of the sun and drop in temperature will have become a lethal icy slope that you will have to descend. If you're un-roped and sliding down a steep gradient, it's very hard to stop once you build up speed.

Wherever possible stick to established trailheads,

which are well signposted, giving you both surer footing and less chance of getting lost. At the time of writing, the accomplished British actor and veteran mountaineer, Julian Sands, is still missing presumed dead after an avalanche may have caught him while he was attempting to climb Mount Baldy in California. Due to high winds, according to the San Bernardino County Sheriff's search and rescue teams, 'the snow has turned to ice making hiking extremely dangerous'. Sands had plenty of experience, gathered over years of climbing difficult peaks around the world. Which shows no one is invulnerable to the caprices of extreme cold weather.

Call ahead to the relevant body – such as the US National Parks Association or the National Trust in the UK – or check the website for a heads-up on the weather. Familiarise yourself with the trail route and always take a physical copy of a route map with you. Before you set out, it's always a good idea to notify someone exactly where are you going and give them an approximate time you expect to be back. Leave a route card that may be used to track your steps, should you happen to disappear. An important thing to remember: it's always better to hike and mountaineer as a group. Also, whether it's a day's climb or walk, make sure you get there early so you're not returning in darkness. Always have a contingency plan if things go wrong.

Case Study: Alive – dine or die

The Old Christians Rugby Football Club is one of the most successful teams in Uruguay. Chartering a plane for players and family, on 13 October 1972, they left Montevideo bound for Santiago, where they would play an exhibition match. When their plane met bad weather they were rerouted to land in Argentina. In thick fog the pilot made a dreadful mistake. Believing them to have crossed to the other side of the mountains, the plane crashed in the Andes. Twelve out of 45 died on impact, with a further five people dying of injuries the following day.

For food stocks they had only two bars of chocolate. On the tenth day of their ordeal, they found a radio and managed to pick up a station only to hear that the rescue search had now been called off and they had all been presumed dead. They refused to allow themselves to give up. Trapped and lost in snowy peaks at an altitude of over 4,000 metres, exposed to temperatures of -35°C, the remaining survivors had a very important decision to make: either they allowed themselves to die of exposure or they did the unthinkable.

Gnawed by malnutrition, they knew that the only source of protein was the dead bodies scattered around the plane. They would have to resort to cannibalism to be sufficiently strong to walk out of there. Since they held him responsible, the players decided to eat the dead pilot first. In the absence of any fire-making tools or materials they were forced to eat raw flesh. Two of the players, Nando Parrado and Roberto Canessa, filled a rugby sock with flesh and headed west. After scaling the first peak to look around and spot the direction of their escape – a green area to which they could head to – they found themselves surrounded 360 degrees by high pinnacles of icy rock.

Roberto's approach to surviving was not to allow himself to look at the mountains ahead of him but just at his feet, allowing him to focus on the task of putting one foot in front of the other, rather than allowing himself to be overwhelmed by the impossible task at hand. I call this the 'one-metre square approach'. As Canessa remembers: 'I decided to take the first step and this is something I've used in the rest of my life ever since. I didn't look at the mountain, I looked to my next step. There are lots of things which I'm certain of in life but unless you take the next step, you will never know how far you can go.'

They finally wandered into a Chilean mountain village, where they were found by a farmer. The main party was found 72 days after crashing. Roberto Canessa has this to say: 'In life, you must all be ready for your plane crash. Life gives us more than we need and we do less than we are able to. We make life more complex than it needs to be; if you have water, food and a bed you have everything you need.'

Instead of losing yourself in negative thinking and the

enormity of a task ahead, try to bring it back to the one-metre square approach, which is about containing the situation and gaining some kind of control of yourself. Don't focus on how far you've got to go, focus on what you're doing, which is keeping moving and occasionally look behind you just to remind yourself how far you've come. Given that your mind has around 70,000–100,000 thoughts every day, much of the time we're unaware of what's going on unconsciously and it doesn't take much for us to be knocked from a positive mindset.

Blizzards

Despite the planet getting warmer, meteorologists believe blizzards will become more commonplace and severe in places where it still gets cold. A blizzard is not just a snowstorm, it can last three hours and more, with freezing, gusty 35mph winds which whip up snow from the ground or falling snow, so there's little to no visibility. The most dangerous element is the freezing temperatures a blizzard brings. If you get caught in one while driving the best thing you can do is pull over to a safe place off the road where another vehicle won't hit you. Cover yourself with blankets and when you get cold, run the engine and heater in ten-minute blasts every hour to warm yourself. To avoid carbon monoxide poisoning, keep a window open a crack to allow sufficient fresh air to get in, and before you hole up for what might be a while until the blizzard stops, check your exhaust to ensure it is not blocked by snow. Do this periodically.

If you're hiking and get caught in a blizzard, seek a treeline or find a natural shelter in the lee of the wind.

Whiteouts

A whiteout is a snowstorm where the precipitation is so heavy that the horizon line between sky and earth become an inseparable mass of white and visibility is non-existent. Although it doesn't have the freezing wind of a blizzard it can be lethal if you try to walk, ski or drive through it.

I remember a story about a father and daughter who were skiing. The girl fell over and her ski slid into a gully. Just when her father had recklessly climbed in to retrieve it, a whiteout occurred. He found himself in what was already a desperately dangerous situation: he was on the side of a gully deep in powder snow which could well be masking a crevasse, his little girl shivering and crying a few feet away. Instead of following his instinct to climb out to reach her, he was smart enough to keep talking to her, reassuring her that the whiteout would soon pass and praising her for not moving. Half an hour later, the sky cleared and they continued to safety (with the ski). You can't fight nature, you must go with it.

Case Study: Ernest Shackleton

Sailing on the good ship *Endurance*, Ernest Shackleton, the quietly spoken explorer, and 27 other brave men set out to become the first to cross the Antarctic continent by foot to the South Pole in 1914. Their mission was to set up camp on the Weddell Sea, from where Shackleton and a few others would then set out to cross the continent and reach the South Pole.

Setting sail from South Georgia, for six weeks the *Endurance* boldly made her way through 1,000 miles of packed ice. Agonisingly, Shackleton and his team were only one day short of reaching their destination when the temperature dropped massively, causing the loose ice to gather and coalesce around the ship. In no time at all she was locked in. One of the men described that as being ‘squashed like an almond in the middle of a chocolate bar’.

Despite the fact it had taken huge efforts to raise the expedition and that this would probably be his last great expedition, 40-year-old Shackleton – his men referred to him as ‘the Boss’ – was by all accounts non-reactive, not losing his equilibrium for a moment. He calmly informed his crew that they would winter where they were while trying to protect the ship splitting in the ice around it. By the end of February 1915, temperatures were falling to below -20°C. Anything superfluous was jettisoned overboard – tools, bibles and the smaller dogs on board, even the ship’s cat was shot.

Come 27 October, any hopes of escaping the ice with the ship intact were dashed. Shackleton wrote: 'After long months of ceaseless anxiety and strain, after times when hope beat high when the outlook was black indeed . . . But though we have been compelled to abandon the ship, which is crushed beyond all hope of ever being righted, we are alive and well, and we have stores in equipment for the task that lies before us. The task is to reach land with all the members of the expedition. It is hard to write what I feel.'

The first attempt to march to the nearest landmass of Paulet Island was soon abandoned when the most distance achieved was a mile per day. Instead, they had to put their faith in where the ice flow took them, but Shackleton knew that any day it was liable to break apart. His misgivings came true on 9 April 1916. Shackleton gave the order to launch the lifeboats as the ice broke up the *Endurance*. Tossed about on the open sea by the belligerent icy waves, the men, some of whom had dysentery and many suffering acute sea sickness, rowed for six days and nights until Clarence and Elephant Islands appeared 30 miles ahead of them.

Their nightmare was anything but over; having landed on *terra firma*, they couldn't have picked a more remote position in which to await a rescue. No ships passed this way, nobody would ever look for them here. Mindful of this, Shackleton – having had only nine days to recuperate from his recent journey in the lifeboat – and a few others set out to try to get help from a whaling station in South Georgia, some 800 miles away. To reach it, they would have to battle huge swells, angry winds and the constant threat of sinking when the boat filled with water. When they finally arrived at landmass, they realised the currents had pushed them off course and they were on the wrong side of the island. In order to get to the whaling station, they would have one more obstacle to navigate: the mountains and glaciers that stood between them and the potential saviours of Shackleton's crew.

On arriving at Stromness harbour in South Georgia, Shackleton lost no time in setting his sights on a rescue mission to Elephant Island, but sadly his first attempt on a whaling vessel made it only as far as the Falkland Islands before having to turn back because of sea ice. The next boat, courtesy of the Uruguay government, came within 100 miles of the marooned crew before it too had to turn back or risk suffering the same crushing defeat from the ice as the *Endurance*. The third attempt was also turned back by the treacherous ice.

On 30 August 1916, as the desolate crew began to lose all hope of a rescue mission, the fourth vessel, a steam tug named *Yelcho*, managed to reach and extract them from Elephant Island back to safety. Not a single man in the entire expeditionary crew was lost.

Ice

Reading ice

Depending on its colour, ice may be sturdy and safe to cross, or thin and treacherous. Blue to clear coloured ice is the thickest to walk on. A thickness of 10 centimetres will support you; 20 centimetres will support several persons, while 30 centimetres of ice will support a Ski-Doo. White to opaque coloured ice indicates thin ice with a layer of recent snowfall over it. Grey, black, slushy ice indicates melting ice and no matter how thick it might seem, avoid it.

Falling through ice

I will never forget when this happened to me, although I went into the freezing water by choice, from a hole we cut into the ice as part of my artic warfare training in Norway. The unit I first joined after passing Royal Marine Commando training was 45 Commando, based in Arbroath in Scotland and considered the arctic warfare specialists. The sensation as I felt my body going into shock, in the coldest water I had ever experienced in my life up until that point, is something that will stick with me forever.

It is imperative that as a soldier who operates in these conditions, you are aware of the drill you must conduct if you suddenly find yourself going through the ice on skis with a full pack and weapon. Also, understanding what will happen to your body when you fall through ice into freezing water is essential. First, your body will experience a cold shock response, something called the 'torso reflex' or the 'mammalian dive reflex' – an involuntary spasm that will force you to gasp for air. It's at this point many drown because they swallow too much water. Some experience a cardiac arrest because of the shock to their system. If you survive these first two scenarios, your heartbeat will have massively accelerated, making you panic.

Slow down your heartbeat, focus on remaining calm and control your breathing. If you're swept under the ice by a current, try to grip onto the passing ice. Then look for the contrasts in the underwater light, as the hole you fell in will radiate sunlight, making the water lighter than the thicker, darker shade of that which is below the ice. Identify that space you're going to head towards and use the ice above you to pull yourself towards the light.

You have much more breath available to you than your body is telling you; when you experience your first torso reflex, that's nature's way of warning you that you're in potential danger, but it's the equivalent of the petrol warning light on your dashboard telling you that your car is almost empty – it's not. Manufacturers build in an early-warning sign so you don't break down in the middle of nowhere before fuelling up again when in truth, most cars can still keep going for at least another 10 miles. The longest anyone's ever held their breath was a 50-something free diver, who apparently reached 25 minutes! So, given that the average person can hold their breath between 60 to 90 seconds without any training, if you can manage to keep your mouth shut during the gag reflex, you'll discover that you have got plenty of air still left in the tank. Obviously, when we are panicking underwater, desperately trying to find our way to the surface, we are not in control of our breathing or heart rate, but a quicker heart rate requires more oxygen. In the split second that the gag reflex occurs, try to master the rising panic, keep your mouth shut and don't breathe out any air.

Your body will lose heat 240 times more quickly in water than in air. The average person can survive in freezing water between 15 and 45 minutes, depending on your level of body fat insulation and fitness. That said, hypothermia will come looking for you within three to five minutes and so your available window to get out before you do yourself critical damage is much shorter.

Reach your arms up out of the water where you fell in and kick with your legs until your torso is out of the water then pull with your arms – don't push down on the ice. Then, once you're fully out of the water, spread your arms and legs to distribute your body weight and roll away from the ice in the safe direction, where you were before you fell.

Once you're on firmer ice that can support you – or, preferably, back on solid ground, take off your clothes in order to increase your core body temperature, wrapping yourself in dry clothes or blankets. If these are unavailable, roll in the snow to absorb the moisture and then try to get yourself out of the wind to a place which is sheltered.

If you can move around to increase the blood flow back to your extremities, then do so. Don't allow your body to come in contact with the freezing surface of the ice; wrap up your feet, body and head. Try to make a fire to warm your wet clothes.

How to save someone who's fallen through ice

Tempting as it may be to run straight to the edge of the ice and pull them out, you don't want to end up in there with them. People drowning will claw their way up on anything in a bid for survival – including you. This is why so many attempted rescues of drowning people result in two deaths, not one. Throw a branch, pole or rope to the person in trouble and approach on all fours or 'swim' over on your belly to spread your weight. If it's rope you're tossing them, tell them to secure it under their armpits and not around their waist before you try to pull them out. To do this, lie on your back, planting your feet wide in the snow and then pull.

EXTREME HEAT

There are essentially two kinds of heat: dry heat, like in the Mediterranean, and humid heat, where there is moisture in the air but it feels sticky. A desert is the perfect extreme of dry heat, just as a jungle is the extreme of humid heat. Which one would you be better off getting dropped into? For me it's the jungle every time.

A jungle is the landscape that just keeps on giving. You have everything you need to survive: plants, live animals, trees, raw materials to build shelters and fires from, and, if you find them, plenty of water sources. A desert, in comparison, is what it says on the tin: deserted. Deserts are all but barren and only the most cleverly adapted lifeforms can thrive in them. You could define a desert as a place that has very little fauna and flora, where the little rain that falls is not retained because of the greater speed of soil evaporation.

The desert

Here's a weird fact for you: one sixth of the world's population lives in arid lands, which themselves account for one quarter of the Earth's landmass. This makes knowing how to survive in one all the more important. Here's how.

Build a fire

I know what you're thinking: why would I want to build a fire if I want to survive in the hot conditions of the desert? Well, with the mercury rising to 50°C, it's not just burning you to bits that a desert excels at; by night, especially during the spring, temperatures drop below zero. To keep warm, look for loose brush or dried animal droppings to fuel your fire. By day, the smoke generated from a smouldering fire will be an effective aerial SOS signal to planes if they are looking for you.

Hydrate

At temperatures of 40°C, the average person loses 900ml of sweat every hour. The sheer force of desert sun will quickly sap your energy and give you heatstroke if you're moving around a lot, so hydrate regularly and take small sips rather than guzzle water. Better still, create a rationing contract with yourself of how often you will sip per hour. You can tell when you're dehydrated and to what level by looking at your urine: if it is lighter in colour then you're not yet dehydrated, but the darker it gets the more serious your level of dehydration. If you do spot some water, check that it is running water and not stagnant. The precious fluids that you have in your body will be wasted on vomiting and diarrhoea in the event you drink some water that is contaminated.

This might sound a bit mad, but if you're running low on water the worst thing you can do is start eating, as the more that you eat, the thirstier you will get. It's OK to have a little nibble for topping up energy but given that the body can survive a lot longer without food than without water (which even in temperate climates is only three days), avoid doing anything that will make you more thirsty.

Build a shelter or find shade

This is one heat you can't fight. Also, the nature of sand makes it very hard to move lightly with little effort. Natural activity in a desert happens during the night so follow the pattern of the wildlife and rest up during the intense heat of the day. Try to avoid the heat as much as possible by creating a shelter out of what you have to hand or can salvage from the environment – ideally something with an entrance and exit for what little breeze there is to be caught by your body. Think back to the shelters in part one of this book (see pages 35–44).

There are many kinds of desert – some have only sand and there are some with rocks, caves, gullies and canyons. Just as you need sufficient shelter to keep out of the sun, you also need lots of layers to keep warm and a small, enclosed space to retain your body heat during the night to prevent you from freezing.

Keep mentally cool

Staying mentally calm and quietening your inner voice is essential. Do not allow it to catastrophise and get you tied up in panic, so you end up pushing off in blind haste, quite possibly in the wrong direction. Instead, focus on breathing steadily and calmly assess your options and your priorities:

- Find a source of water as soon as possible, keeping an eye out for plants or animals. Try digging a well in a dried-up riverbed.
- Focus on what you *do* know about your immediate environment. Do you have any idea which direction is north, or where you currently are? How far away is the nearest known population and in what direction?

- Keeping positive is key: talk to yourself, coach yourself and never give up.
- Set yourself micro targets once you've established that you are heading in the right direction. Remember, identify the Big Dipper/Plough (see page 55) and then look for the North Star and you have found your true north.
- Try to place one foot in front of the other rather than focusing on how far you've got ahead of you.

Keep physically cool

You can't keep a cool head in a difficult situation if you feel like you are on fire. Ensure your head is covered, preferably by a hat with a wide brim to keep your neck cool as well. Cover your head, arms and legs with loose-fitting, breathable clothing and wrap a bandana across your face.

Avoid lying or sitting on the baking-hot desert floor during the day as it this will make your body temperature rocket. Instead, place something between you, at least an inch thick, which can absorb the heat for you. You need to maintain a body temperature of not more than 38.6°C.

See page 77–9 for a reminder on the dangers of heat-stroke and how to avoid it.

Mark your trail

If you're using the cover of night to travel through the desert without a full moon, the chances are you might go the wrong way. Given how precious your limited energy is, you must take all available measures to protect it. Mark your route by building a small cairn to find your way back to if you get lost. In the military we call these ‘waypoints’ and they are vital to getting back on track. During my time as a Special Forces soldier, having emergency rendezvous, making sure we memorised key points in the landscape that we could find our way back to should the shit hit the fan, was an essential part of any mission planning. There’s only one thing worse than the shit hitting the fan and that’s being lost as well when you could have prevented it with a little planning.

A good friend told me a story about a neighbour of his who escaped from Tibet across the mountains into India, where she met the Dalai Lama. When she first came to live in London, she found its Underground map daunting, so walked everywhere. To find her way back through labyrinths of tiny lanes, she left little piles of pebbles on the corners of key streets, like a trail of breadcrumbs.

Animals to look out for in the desert

Snakes:

Death adder, rattlesnake, inland taipan, desert horned/saw-scaled viper, sidewinder and coral snake are some of the potentially deadly or painfully intoxicating reptiles that you could run into in the world’s various deserts. A snake will sense your arrival through the vibrations made by your footfalls and generally move away to avoid you. However, if you surprise them by accidentally dislodging a rock they were hiding underneath or by walking too close to a hole they've climbed into to fall asleep in, then prepare for their wrath.

If you are unlucky enough to be bitten by a snake keep the wound clean and immobilise the affected area. *Never* use a tourniquet to localise the venom. Try not to move as this will cause the venom to disperse more quickly through your body. Keep the affected limb at or below heart level as this will help slow down the spread of the venom. Remove any tight clothing or jewellery near the bite as this will help to reduce swelling. If you feel yourself becoming nauseous or dizzy, or you have double vision or difficulty breathing, this can indicate a severe reaction to the poison. Place a cool compress to the bite to help reduce pain and swelling and seek medical attention immediately. Remaining calm slows down your heart rate, which also helps slow the spread of the poison. If you killed the snake, make sure you keep it with you so a professional can identify the severity of the venom. It could also make for a rather nice trophy – provided you survive.

Scorpions:

Of 1,500 different species of scorpion worldwide only 25 have a sting sufficiently venomous to kill you. The most common symptom from being stung by a scorpion is a sharp burning pain. A more serious sting will spread the pain throughout the body. Bear in mind children and elderly people are more acutely affected as their defence systems are weaker. The worst sting affects the ability of the victim to breathe, swallow and move. Surviving a scorpion bite really depends on several factors, including the species of scorpion, the location of the sting, the severity of the symptoms and the individual's overall health. If you are stung and only have minor symptoms, antihistamine or hydrocortisone cream will help ease the inflammation. If you experience more serious complications, seek immediate medical attention.

THE JUNGLE

As soon as you enter the damp of a jungle your body literally starts to rot. It's difficult terrain to cross, easy to get lost in and very hard to be found. The jungle is neutral and it will always win, but it can also sustain you. For every poisonous thing there's an antidote if you know where to look. It's home to large predators like the jaguar, crocodile, leopard, anaconda and python, and many types of spider and deadly insect. There are plants with sharp spikes that can easily pass through your clothes and into your flesh. The combination of humidity and presence of many bacteria means cuts can quickly become infected. But the main dangers are not just creepy crawlies and big cats; your real nemeses are dehydration, sickness, disease and getting lost. It's vital to drink a lot of water when you're in the jungle as dehydration happens at an accelerated rate here. That said, while it's not difficult to find water, it's a different matter to source clean drinking water. Drinking untreated water that has not been purified is liable to make you feel sick. The jungle is home to tropical diseases like dengue and yellow fever and malaria. Purify the water using iodine or boil it, and remember the basics on water you learnt in Part One (see pages 51–3).

A jungle is literally teeming with life and it's possible to survive a lot longer there than in the desert if you have food, water and medicine. Orangutan babies living in the ever-decreasing rainforests of Borneo and Sumatra remain with their mothers for an astonishing seven years so they can learn the herbal value of plants: which ones can be eaten, which help manage different illnesses and which to avoid; fruits that are edible and those that are poisonous, as well as creatures to avoid. That it takes seven whole years for a baby orangutan to be versed in this gives you an idea just how many things in a jungle can do you harm. But unlike the barren deserts of the world, jungles have more to give if you know what you're looking for.

The jungle phase of my Special Forces training was my favourite, but many of my colleagues absolutely hated it: the impossible humidity that fastens around you like invisible vines sapping you of vital energy, constantly making you sweat, your wet clothes sticking to your body; the giant leeches that seek out the warmth of your crotch and suck your blood while you sleep (sometimes they burrow into your mouth). And then there's the trench foot as your feet start to rot.

Funny things happen while you sleep in the jungle. I heard stories of bugs burrowing into sleeping soldiers' foreheads and laying eggs there, and a few weeks later they had bumps which when sliced open revealed hundreds of baby bugs had been living rent-free inside their heads. There's also an urban myth about a man who fell asleep and woke up to discover a python had swallowed most of his arm, was busily digesting it with its acidic gut while working its way up to devouring his head. Well, there's no myth without fire – it's absolutely true and happened to a Royal Marine soldier during training in Brunei in the Bornean jungle. When they sliced it open, his saviours had to ensure they didn't chop off his hand at the same time.

Key dangers in the jungle

- Heatstroke – take your time, don't rush or over-exert yourself; conserve energy
- Dehydration – keep drinking to top up your fluids
- Mosquitoes – always wear long sleeves and long trousers made of breathable material to protect you from mozzies. Insect bites can easily become infected in the jungle, but more of a concern is that the mosquito is a carrier for dengue fever, malaria and yellow fever. Use the strongest possible repellent available. Alternatively, rub sap from the eucalyptus tree over your skin
- Spiked plants – be careful of getting pricked in the eye

- River rocks – try to go round them if possible; the last thing you want is a broken leg
- Crocodiles – they are found all over the world and vary in size, so beware of swimming in rivers and pools and look out for them when you are collecting water
- Poisonous plants – be careful what you brush against, even the spores from some plants can be harmful.

You can't operate by night when it's dark as there's too much foliage. Instead, you rest during the night. With the many challenges the jungle throws at you, if you've had insufficient sleep, it's lethal, as your body is sluggish and weak and your mind is not on point. In order to give yourself as much sleep as possible, try to have dry clothes you can climb into at night. The jungle places huge demands on the human body; we don't belong there and have long been programmed to fear it for good reason.

Ollie Experience: Jungle messaging

The true measure of a soldier is how well he performs in the jungle. Many who make it this far on selection get beaten when it comes to the jungle survival phase.

Because of its impossibly dense foliage, with every root, branch and vine trying to trip you up, you can't operate at night, so come nightfall, you establish a harbour point and set up your bed system, putting up your hammock and overhead shelter. One of you keeps watch in shifts while the others sleep. As soon as you enter the jungle, your body starts to rot in the humidity, and by the end of six weeks you absolutely stink – in fact, the stench of ammonia is overwhelming. So, before you go to bed you take your wet kit off, which is stinking. You put it in a bag and then you put your dry kit on and it's like luxury beyond anything you've ever experienced, absolute heaven.

But the flipside to this is that come the next morning, by the time the sun first rises over the horizon, you have to have everything packed up and squared away, so you are ready to go, with your bergen on your back and weapons in hand. Dawn is the most likely time for an attack. In pitch black, you have to take off your beloved dry kit, putting it in a dry bag and back into your backpack, and then climb into your stinky old wet kit from the day before. And it is absolutely feral. You do this every day, *every* day, and it's this unbelievably pungent stench.

I hated putting on this cold, damp kit so much that I had to change the internal messaging I was giving myself. Instead of getting negative about this bit of the daily routine, as I climbed into the clothes, I said to myself: 'I love these Armani's. These are the best jeans ever. I look so good in these, oh man!' I wasn't saying it out loud but that's what going through my head, and that's the only way I got through it; I just made it into something else. It was all about reframing, as the clothes were still cold and still wet but I changed my view of them mentally – allowing me to no longer focus on the inconvenience and discomfort of it all.

Jungle predators

If you're in the Bornean jungle, the male orangutan is to be avoided, especially the alpha. You can identify him by the swollen cheek pads around his face – compared to other males the cheeks are much larger as they are inflated with testosterone. This makes him more aggressive and you should avoid making eye contact with him as this will come across as a challenge. A male orangutan is four times stronger than the average man.

You are very unlikely to be chased by a snake in the jungle. You're more likely to stand on one accidentally than be attacked by it unprovoked. Pythons, the longest snakes in the world, are opportunists, but fortunately humans are not usually on their menu. If you see one don't worry, keep your distance and by no means consider picking it up as it will bite you. Its teeth curve inwards so if a python does bite you, you need to take control of its head and carefully remove it, otherwise it will rip your flesh. If a python tries to constrict around you, use your machete on its head and eyes.

King cobras are the largest venomous snake in the

world, they can grow beyond five metres long and have sufficient poison to bring down an elephant. Kings can spit venom over a metre and they will aim for your eyes. It will only attack you if cornered, so if you come across one slowly move away from it.

Found in the jungles of South America, a green anaconda is the biggest snake in the world and can weigh up to 225kg, though they are nonvenomous. If attacked by an anaconda, push your hand down its throat to get it off the snake's fangs. Then, you can remove your hand from the snake's mouth without causing even more injuries as, like pythons, they have curved teeth which act like hooks on their prey. If bitten, slowly open the creature's jaws and vertically pull the fangs out. If an anaconda grips you around the waist, don't breathe in. Poke its eyes or bite its tail to make it let go of you.

Case Study: Lost – the story of Yossi Ghinsberg

Yossi had read *Papillon*, Henry Charrière's moving account of being found guilty of a crime he didn't commit and sent to penal colony for life in French Guiana, South America. Papillon's determination to escape was inspiring and much of it was through thick jungle. Yossi, once he'd finished his national service in the Israeli navy, headed to South America hoping to meet the great Frenchman and retrace one of his jungle routes. Charrière had sadly died, but Yossi made new friends to travel with. One was a teacher from Switzerland, another an American photographer, and together the three men travelled to La Paz, Bolivia. Here they met an Austrian geologist who was planning a journey into the Amazon to look for gold. Yossi Ghinsberg, ever the romantic and naïve to match, begged the geologist to take them, unaware the 'geologist' was a criminal on the run with no idea about jungles and how to survive in them.

They made their way up the Asariamas River where one of them, the Swiss man, Marcus Stamm, developed trench foot. They were walking long distances and to survive they shot and ate monkeys. Stamm refused to eat them so was bereft of energy which, along with his worsening leg, was slowing their progress down. Their supplies were all but depleted and so the self-titled geologist and Stamm decided to abandon the journey and return to base at Asariamas. Yossi and Kevin Gale, the American, continued by making a raft to take them further into the interior jungle. They lost control of the raft in some white water and while the American made it to the shore, Yossi was taken a further half hour downstream by rapid currents. He spent the next four days looking for his friend, who unbeknown to him had been rescued. While Gale spent the next three weeks trying to convince embassies and ambassadors to launch a local search party for Yossi, the Israeli did his best to stay alive against a very hostile environment.

Now he was alone, but not for long. One night he was

almost attacked by a jaguar on the prowl. Using a trick he'd seen in *Live and Let Die* – in which James Bond uses a lit cigar and can of deodorant to create a great fan of flame and kill a snake – Yossi improvised with a lighter and can of lighter fluid. It worked too. Who says Bond films are not educational when you can scare away one of the most fearsome big cats in the world! Next, he almost drowned in a flash flood, then twice was almost swallowed by a bog.

Just when he thought he could go no further, he was joined by a mysterious woman who didn't speak. Yossi tried to take care of her, building her fires and sharing the few berries and eggs he could find to eat with her. She turned out to be a figment of his imagination. Perhaps somewhere deep in his mind something had told his brain to create her in order that he had something else to focus on other than himself in such a desperate situation.

But he still had terrible trench foot, was severely malnourished and his forehead had been burrowed into by worms. Yossi had to cut his forehead open, retrieving 35 worms from inside his head. Because he was slipping in and out of consciousness, he shook a tree full of fire ants to fall on him and wake him up; they bit him all over his body and the pain forced the Israeli out of his delirium. Shortly after, he heard the welcome sound of an outboard motor; his friend Kevin Gale had persuaded locals to help find him in a search and rescue mission. Local people considered it a miracle that Yossi had survived three weeks lost in an uncharted part of the jungle.

If you get lost in the jungle

Jungles are especially easy to get lost in because once you're in one it all looks the same, and with the triple canopy of the trees high above blocking out light, it can be difficult to see. You must always try to stick to the paths and tracks created by humans and animals and stay on the ridge lines away from the overgrown and thick bush areas. Cross graining is when you step off the path and head into the foliage – this should only be done when absolutely necessary, and with the use of a machete to cut your path, using the trees as markers to plan your route forward to avoid going in a circle and wasting vital energy. Traversing by foot through the chaos of vines, tree roots and thick foliage blocking your way is extremely hard work. Add to this the profusion of poisonous plants, some of which only need to lightly brush your skin to release their sting, and barbed thorny plants that can easily create a light wound which has the ability to turn septic in a heartbeat. After a while, because of the endless heat and stifling humidity, your brain starts to lose its grip on reality and you begin to think everything in the jungle has it in for you. It's the ultimate paranoia.

The first thing you must do is stop walking blindly as that's just burning up precious calories that you need to preserve. Remember the breathing techniques we discussed at the beginning of the book (see pages 90–2).

Now that you're calm, try to remember the last thing you noticed – a fallen tree, a stream you crossed, a hill you climbed. If you can't remember any objects, can you recall where the sun was in the sky? Images remind us of things. Use the jungle canopy and the ridgelines as a reference as the jungle floor and foliage that covers it looks very much the same.

Check the ground for any signs of your footprints. It's worth creating a waypoint that you can work your way back to if you think you're going the wrong way. Build a cairn from any readily available materials – it might be a wooden cross you tie to a tree trunk or a pyramid of stones; something you will recognise instantly as your signature.

Picking a direction can be difficult but once you've done so, stick to it. If the light is fading, it's better to stop for the night. Darkness comes very quickly in the tropics, twilight barely gets a look in, so prioritise making a shelter to protect yourself while you sleep. The four key things that you need for the night are:

- Water – collect rainwater in a large leaf and boil if you have the equipment. Bamboo sticks are a useful source of water. Avoid stagnant pools and use your sock as a filter
- A shelter – to keep you dry and safe
- Food – if you're near water, try spear fishing with a two-metre length of bamboo with its end split and separated to act as the spear head. You should avoid eating raw fish so you'll need to have a fire going. Gut the fish, wrap it in a leaf and slowly cook it on stones heated on the fire

- A weapon – use the same technique as for the spear but make it shorter for close-quarter combat.

It's amazing how quickly your senses start to sharpen in the jungle in a way you haven't experienced before; you'll hear things in the busy wall of sound you wouldn't have been able to isolate before and smells become more pronounced, while your night vision will improve within a few days. The American Special Forces used to call it 'purple vision'. During the Vietnam War, specialist jungle warfare operators wouldn't go into sunlight for long periods of time in order to attune their night vision for moving around in pitch darkness.

NATURAL DISASTERS

Natural disasters have been a part of life ever since mankind has been on this fair planet. Our ancestors lived in fear of thunder and lightning, killer waves, volcanoes and earthquakes. To control their deepest fear of these titanic elemental dangers they made gods of each, creating human-like entities to whom they could offer their supplication and sacrifices. In Greek mythology, the unpredictable and ruthless sea became the watery realm of Poseidon, giving fishermen someone they could make their prayers to before a long journey. Just as the Maasai pray to Engai-Narok, the black god, to bring rain to the grassland so they can feed their beloved cattle.

However, for all our modern-day scientific knowledge, the power of the elements is something that we cannot fight. The best we *can* do is understand what to do when natural disasters strike.

Floods and storms

A flood happens when too much water is present in an area for it to drain away normally. Flooding around the world has increased by 50 per cent in the last ten years and kills more people every year than hurricanes or tsunamis. Of all floods, flash floods are the most dangerous as they happen so quickly and often with such violence, washing away houses, buildings, animals and people in their lethal path.

When water levels rise rapidly around you, you need to get yourself to a higher level as soon as possible. Whether it's a tsunami washing inland, a flash flood or a hurricane that has broken through a levee, bringing the river into the city, the higher you are the better.

Flooding can decimate huge areas, making them uninhabitable, with communities left destitute and sick, drinking water sources contaminated by sewage, water-borne diseases rife and the landscape ridden with detritus.

If driving during a flood

There's a reason your local council places signs reading 'Warning: flooding'. That's because most cars are unable to function when immersed in more than a few feet of water.

The rule of thumb is unless you're in a 4x4 with higher clearance, floodwater must not reach higher than halfway up your wheels. Any deeper and it will get into your engine through your exhaust pipe.

If you're indoors during a flood

As the flood rises stay in your building and turn off all water, gas and electricity before heading to the next storey. If you have sandbags and can block or even stem the incoming waters, all the better. If water levels are still rising, you'll need a bug-out bag (see also pages 98–100) to take upstairs. At the very least, you should bring with you spare warm clothing in a dry bag (or knotted refuse bag). Take as much drinking water as you can, as well as torches, batteries, emergency tinned food supplies and dry goods, matches, firelighters, mobile phone, battery booster and some kind of whistle in waterproof, sealed containers.

If flood levels ascend so high you're forced onto the roof, create a makeshift shelter to protect yourself from the rain. Don't wait until you're forced from the roof into the water, try to create some kind of buoyancy raft in advance on which your family can float in advance. If you live in an area which is subject to regular flooding, have an inflatable dinghy handy, as well as an electric/manual pump kept in your attic for such occasions.

Always stay out of the floodwater, remaining dry and safe, as you never know what lies under the water. Realising *during* a disaster that the emergency services are not coming and that you should have taken a little time to consider what the meteorological threats might be to the area you live in is too late. Never rely solely on the emergency services; you'll sleep much better at night knowing that you've got your own emergency plan and kit to deal with it. That's the difference between a victim and survivor.

Case study: Hurricane Katrina

In August 2005, Hurricane Katrina, a level five cyclone packing 140mph winds and 7.5-metre waves, struck America's south-eastern seaboard, aimed directly at New Orleans. As the hurricane laid siege, sanitation and electricity were first to go and the city was plunged into darkness. After eight hours' battery, the assault on the city was far from over. While Americans waited for the lights to return to the houses they had fiercely protected and refused to leave, two levees weakened by storm surges burst and flooded New Orleans, turning streets into canals and eventually claiming 1,800 lives. The devastation caused to one of America's most famous cities and the amount of people who lost their homes and were forced to relocate is forever etched into the Big Easy's history. There are chilling stories of people attempting to flee the disaster being pulled under by alligators. Some families desperately headed to the Louisiana Superdome in hopes of finding protection and shelter, but instead were trapped in a hotbed of crime, where rapes and violence were occurring around them, hopelessly unpoliced. A lack of basic sanitation and bacteria-rich floodwaters combined with 32°C heat created a public health emergency. Eighty per cent of the City of Jazz was underwater.

The weird thing is that the American administration had expected this particular disaster to happen for many years – scientists had predicted that the chances of New Orleans being hit head-on by such a violent storm as Katrina were less than 10 to 1, and yet no adequate preparations were made for such an event. Civil breakdown followed in the wake of Katrina and the administrative response was desperately slow; it wasn't until early September that the National Guard was assembled in sufficient numbers to stem the tide of looting and shooting, not to mention the less than humane way in which the frail, disabled and elderly Black New Orleans residents were left to fend for themselves.

Tsunamis

A tidal wave, otherwise known by the Japanese word tsunami, happens when an earthquake erupts under the sea or when the side of a volcano collapses into the ocean, creating a monstrous wave that moves rapidly, breaking on the nearest landmass. Tsunamis can reach more than 30 metres high. On 26 December 2004 when an earthquake struck with a magnitude of 9.1 off the coast of Sumatra it birthed several tsunamis which rushed across the

Indian Ocean, striking India, Indonesia, Sri Lanka, Thailand and the Maldives. Some 200,000 people tragically lost their lives.

Tsunamis move incredibly quickly, at the same pace as a jet plane. At first, the wave may be small in height but hundreds of miles wide. Just before it makes landfall, the wave hits the shallow water surrounding a landmass and jacks up into the air.

How to survive a tsunami

Since 2004, tsunami warning systems have been much improved, so authorities now know of a tsunami in advance of it hitting. Tsunamis are preceded by earthquakes, so if you're on the coast, you need to find higher ground to ride out the tremors and before the wave arrives. Beware of the sea disappearing on the horizon as if it is being sucked away as it might just seem like the tide is changing from high to low.

The volume of water and detritus a tsunami brings with it is appalling; even the best swimmers shouldn't entertain delusions about swimming it. Sometimes tsunamis make a screaming sound, other times they are deathly silent. If you're on the beach and you hear this noise and see the ocean receding, leaving bare sand and exposed reef in its wake, this is the time you must race as quickly as you can to higher ground. Don't stop to collect anything but your family from the beach.

More than likely, it won't just be one wave, there will

be sustained attacks of successive waves and the water will keep on rising. Again, don't wait for the emergency authorities to tell you there's an emergency, don't wait for the sirens, just follow your instinct. You need to be at least 30 metres above sea level to escape the destruction of a killer wave. If you're unlucky enough to be on a flat island, you need to find the tallest building possible.

Volcanoes

According to the World Health Organization, a volcano is a 'vent in the earth's crust from which eruptions occur'. There are about 1,500 active volcanoes worldwide which affect 6.2 million people. It's not just the lava which seeps from the crater of a volcano which is dangerous, some spew dangerous gases, ash and exploding rocks into the air. Erupting volcanoes can also cause floods, landslides and mudslides if accompanied by rain, snow and melting ice. Depending on how close to the eruption you are, falling ash can cause respiratory diseases, as can inhalation of poisonous gases and fumes. You can also suffer eye and skin irritation caused by acid rain. There is also the danger of getting burnt or seriously injured from rockfalls.

How to survive an eruption

Thankfully, most volcanoes with nearby populations of humans have early warning systems and there are emergency escape plans in place in the event of an eruption. Try to get hold of a hazard zone map, which will illustrate possible paths of lava flows and also give you an idea of how long it takes for the flow to reach different locations.

In the event you are close to the summit of a volcano when it erupts, move away as quickly as you can and don't walk into low-lying areas like valleys, the places where lava flows. To protect your lungs from ash in the air, it's essential you wear goggles and a cloth or a mask over your nose and mouth. Get yourself indoors as quickly as possible. Avoid toxic gases at all costs – volcanic eruptions release sulphur dioxide, which can be deadly. If you smell rotten eggs, leave the area immediately. Ensure all windows, doors, fireplaces, ventilators and aircon systems are locked, sealed and covered up. If you're not in the path of the lava, then hunker down and listen for updates from local authorities on the radio. If you are in the path of the lava, the best way to survive the volcanic eruption is to evacuate immediately and follow the instructions of the local authorities.

Case Study: Surprise eruption

Whakaari, or White Island, is an active volcano some 48km off New Zealand's east coast. In December 2019, a surprise eruption spewed a mushroom cloud of steam, tossing rocks and burning ash into the air, killing 22 tourists. In October and November, scientists had noticed that gas steam and shooting mud from the crater were at their highest levels since 2016. Two weeks before the eruption, an earthquake with a magnitude of 5.9 occurred just 10km north-east of White Island and could be felt as far away as Christchurch.

But strangely, local tour companies were still offering to guide people to the volcano. On 9 December, 47 people were on the island when two short eruptions covered the island in plumes of boiling ash that reached 12,000 feet into the air. Only 25 people managed to get on the waiting tour boats and evacuate. All but three of the survivors suffered serious burns.

Avalanche

An avalanche is a mass of snow known as a snow slide, and while one can start on an incline as mild as 30 degrees, they usually occur at 45 degrees. Once it gathers speed, it can move as fast as 100mph. Around 90 per cent of avalanches are triggered by humans, be it snowmobiles, skiers, snowboarders or climbers. According to the American Avalanche Association (AAA), statistics suggest 93 per cent of victims can survive an avalanche provided they are found and extracted within the first 15 minutes, but thereafter things get a bit sketchy. After 45 minutes only about 20 per cent of victims are still breathing. This is because once the avalanche stops, it settles and solidifies as if it were cement. If you are caught within this, it's very difficult to move.

There are around 100,000 avalanches each year in North

America with around 40 people perishing within them. There are three kinds of avalanche:

- a wet avalanche, caused by the thawing of freshly fallen snow as the temperature gets hotter.
- a soft slab avalanche, caused by snow falling on lee slopes and not settling.
- an airborne avalanche, which begins as a slab avalanche but moves increasingly rapidly the more powder snow it accumulates.

Slab avalanches are responsible for killing more people than any other type of avalanche. It's a horrible way to die; first of all you're tossed about with all the rest of the detritus swallowed up in the avalanche's path, including rocks and uprooted trees, which is moving up to 80mph. If your injuries don't kill you then suffocating in the snow certainly will. Imagine being packed in the hundreds of tons of snow which quickly sets like concrete above you and all around you. At best you might survive for 45 minutes before hypoxia (causing rapid heart rate, confusion and difficulty breathing due to low levels of oxygen) and hypercapnia (an excess of carbon dioxide in your bloodstream causing extreme headache) set in.

How to survive an avalanche

When traversing a slope with a heavy layer of snow, stick to the ridges or ascend to the high ground above any likely avalanche path. Keep an eye out for the gathered detritus of uprooted trees or rocks that will have been carried downhill by the force of a previous avalanche.

The best chance you have for surviving an avalanche is to get out of its path, or at least to the side where the snow is shallower. Try to 'swim' across to the edge of the avalanche as you would to the side of a riptide in the ocean. If you are caught in the middle of the snow stream, try to change your position so your feet are pointing downward, as you'll be sharing the space with rocks and trees. Should you collide with something solid in your path, it's better that it's your feet on the receiving end rather than your head.

Look for something to hold onto which will anchor you, like a tree.

If you get washed *under* the snow, to avoid drowning from inhaling it, protect your nose and mouth by cupping them with your hands and creating an air pocket. Once the avalanche is still, to reorient yourself, spit and watch which direction the saliva falls so now you know to dig your way out in the opposite direction.

Avalanche.org is a useful online tool that tracks avalanche behaviour in North America. If you are in avalanche country it's important that you have an avalanche beacon, a transceiver which broadcasts your location to those trying to find you.

Case Study: A lucky survivor

In 2012, ski rep Rhianna Shaw was skiing off-piste in Austria when a collision with a friend on a snowboard triggered an avalanche and she was swept up in its powerful flow, unable to breathe. Luckily, the avalanche was a short one and came to stop 150 metres down the mountain. In an article in the *Guardian*, Shaw describes trying to breathe as being like 'breathing through a heavy cloth' with snow densely packed around her. At first she thought she was in a dream and then her senses kicked in and she was screaming with panic. Her phone buzzed at her side but she couldn't move her arms to answer it. Shaw thought of the coming summer, which she was to spend with her sister, then began to let go, picturing a forest on either side of her as she calmly walked towards death.

Meanwhile, her friends were searching frantically for her, remembering from their training as ski reps that they had around ten minutes before they would be looking for a corpse. Shaw was not wearing a transceiver and her friends did not have shovels to dig her out, so they had to resort to blindly sticking their hands in the snow. By pure chance, one of them happened upon her leg. Shaw had already stopped breathing when her friend gave her CPR. Her face had gone deathly pale, her lips were blue and her body was suffering from hypothermia. Fortunately, a helicopter was able to rush her to hospital and she survived her ordeal.

Earthquake

The epicentre of an earthquake is the location beneath the surface where the immense amount of energy building up in the Earth's tectonic plates is released. If you imagine the skin of an orange as the Earth's surface, the activity below feels like the fruit moving beneath it. Earthquakes shake buildings, razing them to the ground, and damage gas lines, which in turn cause fires. Seismic aftershocks, which radiate over long distances, create landslides in the form of huge slurries of soil, rocks, water and building rubble. If the energetic rupture is close to the surface, the devastation is worse. Earthquakes occur in three regions: the Mid-Atlantic Ridge, which runs under the Atlantic Ocean; the Alpide Belt, which starts in Eurasia and heads through the Himalayas, Sumatra and Java, and the Circum-Pacific Belt, which follows the edges of the Pacific Ocean and is responsible for 80 per cent of the world's earthquakes as well as 100 per cent of the Earth's deep earthquakes.

The magnitude of an earthquake is measured by a numerical scale known as the Richter scale, which ranges from 1–10. The worst earthquake in history was the Valdivia earthquake in southern Chile, which measured 9.5 on the Richter scale. The quake occurred beneath the sea and created numerous tsunamis which hammered the coast, uprooting buildings and flooding towns and villages. Fortunately, however, a foreshock which preceded the main earthquake had compelled many people to leave their buildings and head for higher ground, saving lives when the main shock hit. The aftershocks were felt as far afield as the Philippines.

There are four kinds of earthquake:

Tectonic earthquake: 5,000 feet below the surface, tectonic plates are constantly rubbing together. When the strength of movement forces one plate under another, this sudden stress causes an earthquake. Most earthquakes happen because of these sliding edges of the tectonic plates, also known as fault lines.

Volcanic earthquake: During a volcanic eruption, pressure that has built up at the base of the volcano due to the formation of magma – molten rock mixed with gas – causes rock to shoot up through the top of the volcano, which spills over with lava. Volcanoes are often found around fault lines.

Collapse earthquake: Collapse earthquakes are smaller and occur when the ceilings of underground caverns and mines fall in. They are caused by seismic waves generated after the main earthquake. They can also be generated by landslides.

Explosion: Human activity like mining, fracking and nuclear explosion can induce this kind of earthquake. If a nuclear device is buried underground in a borehole, huge amounts of nuclear energy are released.

What to do in the event of an earthquake

If you're indoors

If it's a small foreshock you feel beneath you turn off the gas, electricity and water. Don't rush around inside the house once the earthquake has started; it's too late to get outside so find something solid to climb under that will protect you – such as a bed, a table or a desk. Cover your face and head and the rest of your body. Cover your head and body with something protective. If you're at home when the quake starts, be sure to get out of the kitchen, where sharp implements like knives and forks are likely to be falling around and flying through the air. Lean against an interior wall to steady yourself. And if you are hiding under something, make sure you hold onto it with one hand so you are both moving at the same time. With the other hand, cover your head and body.

If you're outside

Being outside close to buildings which are being shaken with such force they may fall to the ground is the worst place you can be. If you're outside, try to head to an open place where there are no big trees or buildings that can collapse on you. Be as observant as possible. Are you near a telegraph pole or a power line? Are you on the coast at sea level? There's every chance that the eruption will cause a tsunami, so you haven't got long to head up to higher ground or get as far inland as possible. If you're in mountainous country, watch out for falling rocks. A storm drain is a good place to hide.

If you're out shopping, stay away from the windows of the store and find something you can shield yourself under. Make sure you're a safe distance from shelves and anything heavy that could fall on you. If you happen to be in a lift, get out as quick as you possibly can. These things go down!

If you're driving

Pull over to the side of the road, making sure you're not blocking the route. Stay in your car with the radio on so you can hear what the emergency services tell you to do. It might sound like common sense but make sure you're not parked under an underpass, overpass or any other kind of bridge. If you see an electric live powerline snaking around, don't go near it, stay in the car. There will be aftershocks.

Wildfire

A wildfire is an inferno which burns uncontrolled in a natural area, sometimes swallowing thousands of acres of land and taking lives, homes, pets, businesses and wild animals. Wildfires require three components to complete their deadly triangle: a heat source (lightning bolt, humans leaving campfires unattended, etc.) to ignite the flames; fuel (dead trees, grasses and living vegetation) to keep it going, and oxygen and wind to feed the fire and help it to spread. Because of global warming and climate change, potential hotspots are now so much drier and therefore more prone to burning. Average wildfire season is now three months longer than it used to be just a few decades ago. According to *New Scientist*, 'As rising greenhouse gas emissions are increasing droughts and heat, more catastrophic wildfires are expected in the years to come, especially with the fire season getting longer.'

Heat waves have become part of the modern vocabulary. The UN predicts that by 2030, there incidences of wildfires will increase by 14 per cent. In the US, a staggering 85 per cent of forest fires are thought to be caused by humans, be it from burning rubbish which then gets out of control, tossing lit cigarettes into dry stubble, acts of arson and the biggest cause: campfires left unattended. Nature is also responsible for igniting forest fires with lightning bolts.

In the first half of 2022, wildfires destroyed huge swathes of land on a level previously unseen. It's no longer just in California and the Australian bush where wildfires are getting worse; European countries like Germany, France, Spain, Greece, Portugal, Italy and Croatia have also lost land to fire on an unprecedented level, with three times as many fires occurring than the previous average. The horrendous fires of late 2019 and 2020 in the Australian bush are some of the worst wildlife disasters in modern history – 181 million birds, 51 million frogs, 61,000 koalas and nearly 140 million other native mammals were consumed by the flames in an area roughly the size of England.

Ten years ago, we witnessed the peat fires in the Indo-Bornean jungle which decimated orangutan populations as well as a great many other rare species. This was a direct result of the palm oil industry forcing its way into the natural lungs of the planet and lighting fires to clear away ancient trees to make room for farming the fruit. Rainforests store carbon dioxide and when they are burnt, they release carbon monoxide (CO_2) into the Earth's atmosphere, where it gets stuck, blocking the escape of UV rays from the sun, causing the greenhouse effect, which heats up the planet. Now the size and frequency of wildfires are growing, devastating ecosystems and impacting the weather and health of the earth's inhabitants.

What to do if you're caught in a wildfire

If you're outside

Easier said than done but try to stay calm. Remember that you can't outrun a forest fire; with the wind behind them, they move as swiftly as a galloping horse. If you can smell the fire but still can't hear or see it, take a moment to assess your best escape route. The worst place you can be in an advancing fire is up a hill or downwind of it. If from a distance you can see the smoke and the way it is being blown, head in the opposite direction. If the wind is blowing straight towards you, run in a perpendicular direction to avoid the flames.

If you can't get out of its way in time, check on your phone or map for a lake, pond or river nearby that you can reach to immerse yourself in the water. If there's no water near enough, you need to find an alternative natural firebreak, like a gorge, cave or a clear area among rocks. If the fire is close and you're in its path then try to find somewhere with very little vegetation (poor fuel for the fire). Then, with a moist cloth over your mouth, lie low to the ground to avoid inhaling CO_2 smoke, cover your body with a wet blanket/soil and stay there until the fire passes by. The biggest killer in a wildfire is smoke inhalation.

If you're inside your house

Call the emergency services. If there's time, remove any flammable objects from around the house, like stacks of firewood or recycling, and if you've got an outside oil tank, make sure that any brush or long grass which may have grown around it is cut down so there's no fuel for the fire to reach it. Before you bed down inside collect as many large containers as possible and fill them with water, making a ring around your perimeter. This wall of water may slow down the fire.

Once inside, fill up your sinks and baths with cold water in the event that your water supply is restricted or completely cut off. Shut off the oxygen supply to the house to rob the fire of fuel by closing ventilation fans in the kitchen and bathrooms. Close all doors and move curtains away from windows, having ensured they are all tightly shut. Put all the lights on if it is night so your rescuers can see where you are. Stay away from outer walls and windows that will eventually smash in intense heat. The longer they are intact, the less oxygen is available for the fire so don't break them yourself in an attempt to release smoke.

If you're driving

Only drive if the smoke is not so thick that you can still pick out the road ahead of you. Keep all the windows shut, close off all ventilation entry points and drive slowly with your headlights on so other cars can see you. If your visibility is so limited by smoke that you can't continue, stop the car in a place as clear as possible of trees that may fall on you. With the fire coming towards you, you might be tempted to leave the vehicle and run in the opposite direction, but again, don't even think about it, as the smoke will have an immediate effect on your lungs and render you unconscious. Even though the car may be shaken by the hot air currents and the temperature is ratcheting, it is cooler in the vehicle than it is outside. Your chances of survival depend on you remaining in the car. Lie low on the floor, covering yourself in a blanket or coat, and use a wet handkerchief or bandana around your mouth to prevent smoke particles from entering your lungs.

Creating a fire break

If you can starve the fire of fuel in your vicinity by burning any flammable material before it arrives, you may save your life and others with you. Only attempt this if the fire is still reasonably distant. The first thing you must do is clear a perimeter around you a minimum of 10 metres wide. Remember that because of the wind, the fire will be able to leap and reignite, thanks to airborne burning embers. First, mark out the break and then light your fire, burning any flammable material like branches, leaves and long grass so that there's nothing left to feed the wildfire. The idea is that the fire, not finding anything with which it can sustain itself, will go around you.

Tornado

There are three kinds of tornado: multiple vortex (two or more spouts occurring at the same time), land spout (land-based twister) and water spout (forming at sea). What causes a tornado? When heat rises and cool air descends in a thundercloud and the two meet, it can cause spinning air currents which drop down to ground level in a vertical spout still connected to the cloud. Also known as twisters, these violent funnel-shaped columns of air can last between 10 minutes and an hour and destroy everything in their path, with 300mph winds seizing and tossing livestock as if they were Jelly Babies, smashing houses and barns like toothpicks. The longest, most fearsome tornado ever recorded was the Tri-State Tornado of 1925, so-called because it's stretched over three states (Missouri, Illinois and Indiana). Travelling at incredible speeds, it lasted three and a half hours and covered 219 miles. The best known area for these meteorological pitbulls is Tornado Alley, a huge area which extends from Texas to Ohio, covering Iowa, Kansas South Dakota, Oklahoma and Nebraska in between.

If you're outside

Given that tornadoes form among storm clouds, be vigilant for green-tinged thunderheads and the roaring sound of jet planes which accompany the funnel. Even in your car you are not safe and should try to drive to the nearest building and hunker down inside. Drive away from the twister at a right angle to its path. If you are caught short, without a car and nowhere to run and hide, look for the nearest ditch to lie flat in, covering your head and face to protect yourself from falling debris.

If you're inside

Try to find a room without windows in the lowest level of the house/building. If there is a basement, head down there. Lie down beneath a solid table or mattress and protect your face with your arms. Avoid using a lift. Avoid high-rise buildings and those with flat roofs. Stay put in your shelter and keep abreast of local news stations. Even after you think the twister has passed, going outside might not yet be an option, as there could be multiple twisters at work in your area.

PART FOUR:

PERSONAL CRISES

BEREAVEMENT

Grief is a natural response to loss. We can grieve the loss of health, the death of a pet, the end of a relationship, retirement, the passing of a loved one. Death is a feature of life and as sure as the sun will rise tomorrow, we all have an appointment with the Grim Reaper sooner or later.

Our first experience of death is often our grandparents, though if you are in the Armed Forces there's a good chance you may witness somebody being killed in the field before your grandparents pass. I think that in the West, we need to create a healthier relationship with death, viewing it not as the end but rather a gateway to the next place.

The loss of a loved one is a deeply unsettling and emotionally troubling experience. It gives rise to a spectrum of feelings, from sadness, anger and guilt to confusion and depression. It can have a serious effect on your mental and physical health if you try to deny it space. Grief is a passageway that we must walk down in order to heal. A big part of healing is allowing yourself to cry, which in itself is an inbuilt vital human mechanism which helps us cope. It releases biological chemicals in our bodies which help us feel lighter after we've had a good weep.

We get to know ourselves better when we go through pain. Pain is a natural feature of life and a component of the healing process. The great nineteenth-century firebrand philosopher Friedrich Nietzsche believed that it was only through pain that we could come to know our real selves and that only through pain and adversity could a person find wisdom and inner peace. The pain we experience through grief, then, is part of what makes us human and real and gives us substance. The biggest tragedies in our life offer us the greatest lessons from which we can evolve. '*Amor fati*' means to 'love your fate', accepting whatever joys, hardship and pain it brings you. Look at the most painful episodes in your life – what vulnerabilities did they reveal to you? What knowledge have you gained and how can this knowledge prepare you for similar things in the future? These tragic events haven't killed you, they have made you stronger.

When we push down trauma in order not to give it a voice, it comes back to haunt us further down the road. We need to sit with pain and allow it to follow its course. Eventually, through tears and time, it will pass, but it should never be rushed. There will be good days which bring a sense of acceptance and peace, but that doesn't mean you won't suddenly be plunged back into your sadness and loss another day.

Grief is often viewed as having five stages:

- Denial
- Anger
- Bargaining

- Depression
- Acceptance.

There is no particular order in which these emotions will appear, other than acceptance, which is the final destination of the process, when we move on with our life again, forever changed but at peace.

The symptoms of grief

Grief has many faces and all of them are perfectly normal.

- **Shock and denial** – it feels as if you've been hit with a sledgehammer and the rug has been pulled from under your feet. Many of us go to a place of denial and disbelief because we find it impossible to accept that a person who we love is no longer there.

- **Guilt** – life is never perfect and death can be unexpected and sudden. You may feel regret for things that you wished you'd said and now can't, or something you said that you wish you could take back. Or perhaps you experienced a sense of relief when the person passed away and you feel like this is a 'wrong' reaction

- **Sadness** – emptiness and despair are the foot soldiers of sadness; perhaps you are distant towards others or constantly in tears

- **Fear** – if it's a parent or a partner who made

you feel safe when they were alive, you may feel insecure and helpless with their passing

- **Anger** – perhaps you feel abandoned by the person who's passed on or maybe you feel rage towards the world and those around you.

Physical symptoms of grief

- Fatigue
- Nausea
- Weight loss or weight gain
- Insomnia.

Ways to deal with grief

- Talk about it with somebody you trust
- Start a journal in which you express your sadness and appreciation of the person
- Take good care of yourself – eat healthily, get plenty of exercise, reach out to your support network and don't be afraid to let people know you feel vulnerable and down
- Consider joining a support group for people who have experienced a similar loss
- Honour your loved one's memory by creating a memorial. Or hold a candlelit vigil or plant a tree in one of their favourite places
- If grief is affecting your daily life and heavily

impacting on your relationships, then it's a good idea to seek the help of a therapist or counsellor

- Remember there is no calendar to grief, it lasts as long as it lasts
- Keep busy
- Don't let anybody tell you how you should be feeling.

ADDICTION

According to Canadian psychiatrist Dr Gabor Maté, 'Addiction is manifested in any behaviour that a person finds temporary pleasure or relief in but suffers negative consequences as a result of and does not give up, or can't give up, despite those negative consequences.' The greater the suffering of the trauma in our youth, the stronger the addiction will be in later life. Addiction is a kind of self-medication, an attempt to find escape from suffering. The area of the brain that experiences physical pain is the same as experiences emotional pain. Drugs like marijuana, cocaine, heroin and alcohol not only possess mental but physical pain-relieving qualities. They work in the human brain because they act like natural chemicals produced in our body called endorphins. Endorphins regulate the gut, the immune system and provide the brain with pain relief, as well as making possible experiences of joy, pleasure and reward. The third function of endorphins is love, defined as the attraction which drives two bodies together with an attachment to take care of one another.

Dopamine, another vital chemical produced by the brain, is an incentive motivator and is released in the seeking phase of hunger or in the search for a sexual partner. Dopamine gives us feelings of happiness and euphoria, the feeling of being alive. Gambling, sex and shopping addiction all produce high dopamine levels.

Scientists believe that the brain develops under the impact of its environment. The most important ingredient in the formation of a healthy-minded adult is the quality of the parent-child relationship that they experience at a very young age. Not surprisingly, consistent parenting where the mother and father are happy, non-stressed, approachable and responsive produces the most balanced people in later life. These conditions have to be present in the child's environment in order for their facets of self-regulation, stress regulation and emotional equilibrium to function normally.

We all carry a level of brokenness within us and yet this brokenness is part of what makes us human. Your experiences in your formative years as a child shape who you become as an adult. After my father left, almost overnight, we experienced a massive shift in our finances, going from being a wealthy family to one that was struggling. Money went from being something we'd always had and tookfor granted to something we worried about and feared. These sorry undertones of loss carried on into adulthood – no matter how much I earned, I never seemed to have enough – and harked back to the sudden *lack* I experienced as a child.

The essence of trauma is disconnection from the self, something I have experienced throughout my life as an addict, trying to heal the wound I couldn't see or touch with the aid of alcohol or drugs. Violent trauma to the skin results in scar tissue growing over the wound like hard webbing. Unlike normal skin, it's not flexible but rigid and masks feeling. The same can be true of deep trauma to the emotional self and the resultant loss of feeling.

How to beat addiction

Recovering from any addiction is a lifelong journey but with the right support and resources you can survive and thrive in recovery.

- The first step in recovering from addiction is admitting that you have a problem and that you need help.
- Seek professional help through a counsellor, therapist or an addiction specialist, all of whom can provide you with a personalised treatment plan and support you in your recovery.
- Join a support group – groups such as Alcoholics Anonymous (AA) and Narcotics Anonymous (NA) provide you with a community of people who understand exactly what you're going through and can offer encouragement and support.
- Change your environment. We are a product of the people we have around us, so remove yourself from those who enable your addictive behaviours,

instead surrounding yourself with supportive people who will be there for you.

- Practise self-care – look after your physical and mental health by eating a balanced diet, exercising regularly and getting enough sleep. Engage in beneficial activities that bring you joy and relaxation, such as meditation, yoga or reading.
- Set a timeline for quitting, telling your friends and family so they can support your goal
- Be aware of habits, people and places that trigger your addiction. The better you get to know your triggers, the easier it is to avoid them. Stress is often a trigger for many addictions and can be managed with meditation, a walk in nature or using aromatherapy.
- Keep your distance from the object of your addiction – if it's drugs, alcohol or co-dependence that you're trying to withdraw from, remove the temptation by avoiding the person, place or party environment in the beginning. As time goes on and you become stronger, exposure to them will not be such a problem as your resistance grows.
- Taking responsibility and being accountable for your actions is paramount. Consider working with a therapist or counsellor, or ask a trusted friend to help you stay on track in your recovery.

- Overcoming addiction is not a sprint but a marathon and you need to be prepared that in the early days of your recovery you may slip and fall. Cut yourself some slack; setbacks are a part of your journey.
- Cognitive behavioural therapy (CBT) is an approach that focuses on identifying and changing thoughts and behaviours which play a part in addiction. It has been very effective in helping people overcome all kinds of addictions.
- Mindfulness therapy is helpful for people with underlying mental health problems like anxiety or depression. Thoughts give rise to feelings and if we can learn to control those then we can begin to control our inner voice.
- Write down the reasons that you want to change, imagining how much better your life will be once you've overcome your addiction.
- Make a list of positive things you want in your life that overcoming your addiction will help to bring you. For example: a dream job, better health, more money, more time with friends and family, a sense of freedom.

Managing withdrawal symptoms

Withdrawal symptoms are a difficult aspect of overcoming addiction, for both substance and behavioural addictions.

With substance addiction, physiological aspects of withdrawal can be very uncomfortable. Remember that the whole purpose of an addiction is to anaesthetise that inner emptiness and fracture, an attempt to paper over what is a painful wound, therefore it's only natural that when you take the self-medications away, you're going to feel exposed and raw. The most acute symptoms of withdrawal pass within a week or two of quitting, be it nicotine, sex addiction, pornography or taking drugs. Forewarned is forearmed so speak to a doctor or a counsellor who can tell you what to expect in the first days of abstinence and support you on your journey.

Relapsing is not a sign that you failed, it's part of your journey and the recovery process. Around 40 to 60 per cent of people trying to overcome substance use disorder will relapse at some point.

The purpose pyramid

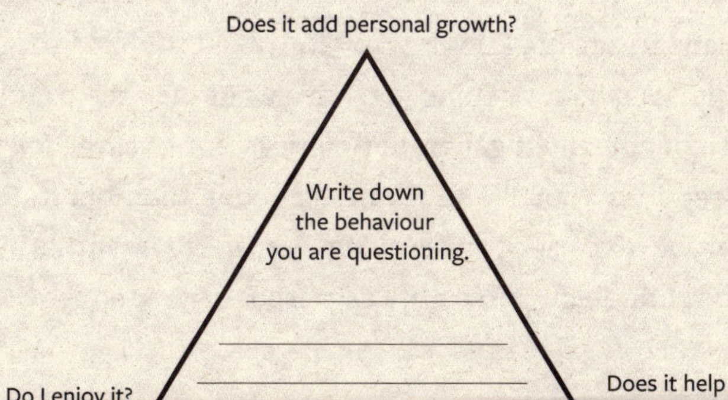

The purpose pyramid is a useful tool to measure the worth of anything in your life that may be of questionable merit. Draw a triangle and at the top of it write, 'Does it add personal growth?'. On the bottom left point write, 'Do I enjoy it?'. And on the bottom right, write, 'Does it help others?' In the middle of the triangle write down the behaviour you are questioning. In the case of dependence and addiction, this is the substance or habit, but you can use this pyramid to look at the value of other things in your life, like a job, a relationship or even a travel plan.

Then work your way around the triangle clockwise. If alcohol is what you are questioning, you will ask, 'Does alcohol add personal growth?' In my case the answer is a firm no; it just adds destruction and negativity, and is a time waster. The next question, 'Does it help others?' Certainly, it doesn't help me or my family, as I end up being the worst version of myself, grumpy and self-loathing, which is a bad place to operate from. And finally, 'Do I enjoy it?' Do I like the three days of muddy headedness and depression? I'd have to say no, I don't enjoy it.

The behaviour or thing you have written in the centre of your triangle must generate two ticks out of three for you to keep it in your life. If it only gets one then bin it. Each time you experience a craving during your withdrawal, keep reminding yourself of the purpose pyramid.

JOB LOSS

Losing a job can be a blow to your self-esteem and confidence, particularly if it's one you've held for years, as well as sending you into a panic as you try to figure out how you are going to pay for everything: from the rent or mortgage, lease payments on the car, to holidays, the weekly shop and travel costs. You might realise just how many extravagant outgoings you have, but also how many critically necessary ones too. Your mind will be running at a million miles an hour as you attempt to figure out how you are going to find the money to pay all these bills and support your family.

Some of us have a contingency fund, a dedicated cache of money to be used only in real emergencies. Maybe it's a few thousand to get us through a couple of months if we become ill or lose our job. Maybe we've been putting our annual bonus in the fund for the last couple of years. An emergency fund is a safety net that cushions our fall while we get ourselves back on our feet and find a new job. But what if you haven't been so careful or weren't earning enough to be able to put money aside each month? It's nothing to be ashamed of – life is expensive. Panicking will achieve nothing but send you into a state of depression and anxiety. In this state, it's very hard to get anything positive done. Breathe and try to be calm, reminding yourself that you have faced tough difficulties in the past and have survived to tell the tale. Perhaps look on it as a blessing in disguise, as a silver lining to a cloud because it represents new opportunities and a chance to grow. Tell yourself that things happen for a reason and try to trust that there is a process at work and in the long run, it will be better.

It starts with a plan

Write down everything which is a debt or an outgoing, so you know exactly what you have going out of your accounts. Next, go through these outgoings and start deleting the things which you can do without, leaving just the essentials. Now look at these essentials and see if you can make any cheaper, perhaps switching to a less upmarket supermarket chain for your groceries or shopping around for a new electricity and gas supplier. In this way, you're beginning to build a transparent and honest audit of your finances, hopefully managing to reduce the burden somewhat.

Creating options

Next, consider short-term options to keep you afloat. Banks and financial institutions are more than happy to offer you a bigger overdraft when they see a regular flow of income to your account – basically, when you don't need it – but the moment you're in trouble, they're strangely reluctant to help. Rather than take out an interest loan which may get you in deeper water, consider if there's a family member who may be able to lend you some interest-free money to keep you buoyant for a couple of months while you're hunting for a new job.

Don't allow yourself to wallow in self-pity. Your new modus operandi should only involve looking for work. Where attention goes energy flows, and just by being proactive - sending your CV out, networking and keeping busy - you're sending yourself a message of self-respect as well as putting yourself on the radar of prospective employers. Focusing on your physical and mental health is critical. Make sure you eat well, with food that gives you long-lasting energy rather than short-lived spikes. Get enough sleep. If you find yourself lying awake worrying at 3am, then before bed each night, write down the things that are bothering you and go through possible solutions in your mind. In this way, they won't haunt you when you're trying to give your brain and body a rest. Don't let job loss get you down, focus on remaining positive and moving forward. Try not to be a hero and take it all on your own shoulders; share it with your partner, family and friends and let them support you through it.

Try to see what's happening as an opportunity to find a job that will really satisfy you. People who are fired or made redundant often feel like they are failures because they didn't achieve everything they wanted to in their previous roles. Do not let this feeling define your entire journey after a job loss. Instead, focus on what you can do to improve your career prospects.

It's important that you don't rush into the first new job

opportunity that presents itself, doing the same as your last role. There may be a reason why you've been let go; perhaps you were coasting because you weren't happy. Focus and visualise what you really want to do with your career to identify the perfect job for you. What does it look like? Put some clay on it: imagine your office, what you would be doing and how you can make a difference.

Social media sites like LinkedIn are useful networking tools, allowing you to increase your profile and connect with potential employers. Check out the company websites you are interested in; follow their latest news and developments so you have something to refer to when you write to them. Grow your online visibility. Each week, create a roadmap with a desired place you want to get to by the close of that working week. Make lists, update your CV, agree with yourself the number of letters you wish to send out every day. Keep reaching out to your professional network. Consider upskilling or reskilling. Get excited about your next job.

Case Study: Rolling stones gather no moss

I know of a CEO who had been earning well over £100,000 a year and lost his job. His monthly outgoings were huge. The following week, he found a new job stacking supermarket shelves and another working as a barista in a café. He knew himself sufficiently well to realise that if he just sat at home waiting for the phone to ring, he would lose himself in a spiral of depression, self-loathing and panic, and nothing would be achieved. To be in the right place mentally where he could look for jobs, he needed to keep himself busy and sane. He was earning just enough to get by, but sadly that still wasn't enough, despite having a contingency fund. He had to take a further step of taking one of his sons out of boarding school until he could balance the books to support the household. Eventually, he got a new CEO job, but the point of the story is that he cut his cloth according to his present means, took on no new debts and kept himself sufficiently busy to keep depression at bay and find a new job.

PART FIVE:

AGGRESSION

PHYSICAL ATTACKS

In 2020/21 there were 235 murders in England and Wales involving a knife or sharp object and over 40,000 offences involving a knife were reported to the police. Anti-crime measures are failing to improve the situation. Many of the knife wielders are teenagers, as are the victims. Much of the problem is rooted in gang culture, where unnecessary pride and hot tempers can make a situation flare up very quickly. Thanks to austerity cuts, there are now 20,000 fewer police officers on the streets in the UK, as well as a dearth of youth workers who can guide troubled young people and teach them that a knife will not protect them.

When we are confronted by danger our pupils dilate and focus on the object that is causing the threat and our heart and respiratory rate increase so we can run, fight or hide. Glucose is released into the bloodstream to allow more energy to our cells and our blood flow is shunted to the extremities, away from our internal organs so we can react quickly. Adrenaline and cortisol flood the muscles so we can fend off our enemy; circulation moves from the rational forebrain to the back brain, reducing our capability to think creatively, instead relying more on instinct to react effectively to the threat facing us. When we're not stressed, our forebrain can handle around five to nine bits of information at any time, but when stressed, that goes down to one or two. This is why in these situations, the more you try to think, the more stressed and confused you'll be. It is essential you establish a good breathing pattern to reduce the overstimulation of cortisol and give you a mindset of clarity and not confusion.

I remember all too well the situation on the highway in Iraq when I was attacked while escorting VIPs to Baghdad. The militia sprang the ambush at speed and in that moment, when it became clear that the vehicles behind us meant business, I shat myself! Not literally of course but I had never felt the intensity of that fear before, nothing close! For the first time in my life (apart from when I was attacked by the chimp), I had no supporting assets around me, no highly trained team with the best weapon systems you can imagine. It was just me and my number two sat behind me, against two vehicles full of militia.

Everything happened so fast and the incident was dense with predominantly negative mental activity. I started focusing on all the things that could go wrong, based on intelligence reports of beheadings at the side of the road. I started to panic about my responsibility for the 12 people in the three vehicles in front of me, who were relying on me to keep them safe. But as soon as I heard the intimidating sound of the multiple AK47s firing, something in me sparked. My training kicked in and everything that happened after that was instinctive. I immediately realised what I had to do and that was to strip away everything

I couldn't control, let go of my worries about the VIPs in the front vehicles and disregard all the things that could go wrong. What I needed in that moment was to deal with the threat that was imminent – the cars behind.

I gasped for air like I'd not breathed in the last minute and immediately felt mental clarity return. In that moment, I gave the order to open fire as I aggressively took the vehicle to the next lane over. They fell for the trap and moved into the position to my left as I raised my MP5 Kurtz on my left arm. I was staring down the barrel of an AK47 and squeezed off a burst of automatic fire into the enemy car. The car bounced into the central reservation and we increased speed back home to the compound as we saw smoke billowing from the car.

If I hadn't managed to control my faculties, I believe I wouldn't be writing this book. Understand that in any situation where there is a threat to your life or your safety, your mind is the best weapon you have.

When someone threatens you with a knife, it's likely that instinct will take over and one of three things will happen. Your brain, in absolute panic, may click into something known as 'flight', giving you the necessary adrenaline rush to get you out of there as fast as you can. Alternatively, your instinct may tell you that the only way you're going to survive this is to fight your way out. To do this, your brain will release a shot of testosterone, making you stronger and more fearless, but this might not be helpful, as if you are not experienced with disarming someone wielding a knife, there's a good chance you could get yourself killed. The third response is known as 'freeze mode', which is when your mental system is so overloaded with panic (produced by overstimulation of cortisol, which promotes stress) that you stand there rooted to the spot.

None of these states are helpful and will escalate matters further. What you need to do is try to remain calm. Breathing deeply, in through the nose and out through the mouth, helps earth you and stops your voice tremoring. Your hands are probably going to be shaking because this is so out of your comfort zone and unfamiliar.

The reason thugs usually get the better of people who are stronger physically than them is because they have lost the fear that most of us possess of getting hurt or of the consequences of hurting someone else. And it's a good job that 99 per cent of humans have an inbuilt reluctance to fight, otherwise there wouldn't be many of us left as we would've all killed each other. A scrapper, hooligan, thug, whatever you want to call them, gets in enough fights for that pause button to no longer work; that fear of being hurt or of hurting others carries no threat because they are so familiar with it. They don't experience the jelly legs and milky feeling of dread in the gut that most men and women get prior to a fight, which renders them frozen and makes them back down, perhaps because their body no longer produces those cortisol warnings as they've survived previous fights.

An example of this is when I started jumping out of

helicopters for a living. Called fast-roping or rappelling, it's pretty hairy, with your life flashing past you as the ground speeds towards you at 2.5 metres per second, the rope whistling through your gloved fingers. Your hands are used as the brake and when the ground starts to look pretty detailed you slow down, though the last thing you want to do is become a 'dope on a rope', hanging in mid-air like a sniper's dream. It's a fast and aggressive action that at first sends the body into a paroxysm of fear because you're basically asking it against all common sense to leap out of a helicopter with just a rope; it's madness. But each time you successfully don't expire, it dilutes your inbuilt fear until there is none and you could almost do it in the dark onto a moving target at sea – which is exactly what I specialised in with the Special Boat Service.

Another example is when you start sparring as a boxer. The first hits you take to the face and head can send you into freeze mode because your body just doesn't know what to do. It doesn't want to hurt another person. Some people's eyes fill with tears and it's got nothing to do with being sad. It's only by chipping away at the shield of resistance to hurt others that the fledgling boxer begins to throw their own shots and develops as a fighter.

The short and fast is that unless you have some sort of experience in self-defence or sparring, or have practised a martial art, being attacked without warning will be so far away from anything you've experienced before that remaining calm is not a possibility. You only develop calm when you know what you're doing in a fight and can handle yourself, which enables you to think and slow your racing mind so you can control the situation. Arguably, if you possess the confidence in yourself to fight back this will be reflected in the way your body carries itself before the attack. On a purely animal level, a thug sizing you up will be less inclined to mess with you if you radiate calm, hold yourself with confidence, walk with purpose and are not afraid to look them straight in the eye.

Making the first move and seizing the initiative

A friend of mine used to be a travel writer and often worked in far-off places. One night on a dark beach in southern Cambodia, he was tramping through the sand towards a distant light on the shore (the guesthouse he was staying in that night), a heavy pack on his back. Unbeknown to him was that Otres beach was renowned for shootings and muggings, especially lone travellers at night. Just the week before, someone had been killed.

He was exhausted from travelling on a rattly bus with no legroom for eight hours but sufficiently awake to keep his vigilant mode operating a little while longer, at least until he was safely at his destination. He started to feel uneasy and looked around for evidence of why that might be so. He spotted two figures in the darkness some way behind him. Each time he turned around they seemed to be five steps closer to him. Eventually, he could pick out their faces: they were a couple of young men. Either they were playing 'What's the time, Mr Wolf?' and they had neglected to tell him, or they were closing in on him to mug him.

He looked back beyond the youths to a beachfront hotel he had walked through, concluding to himself that this was where they'd probably noticed him; he then gazed ahead at the distant light of where he was going, too far away to run to. Pretty soon they would make their move; it was just a question of time before it got to the stage of them showing their claws and getting a knife or gun out. Instead of allowing it to get to that, he chose to do something unpredictable. He put down his backpack, made himself look bigger by squaring his shoulders, walked as calmly as he could to his pursuers until they were almost nose to nose and shone his torch directly into their faces, all the while holding their gaze with his own and smiling. He stood there a few seconds and, spooked, they turned around and walked away into the night. There was no aggression, just a show of confidence, however fabricated it might have been. He didn't shout or throw a punch; he just took the first move to them, which they hadn't been expecting, and projected a sense of confidence and power. Then he allowed himself a big sigh of relief and carried on.

An attacker wielding a knife

Try to deescalate the situation by assuring your attacker that you don't want any trouble and just want to go on your way. Tell them if it is money they want, they can have it. Don't make any sudden moves, keep your manner calm and neutral. Take deep breaths and maintain eye contact. You wouldn't take your eyes off a cougar stood above you, ready to pounce, would you? Because right at that moment the cat is assessing whether he's going to fight you or not, the smallest indication you are weak, like a loss of eye contact or turning your shoulder as if to take flight, suggests you are more scared than it and the cat will strike. In much the same way, don't allow your eyes to drop with someone holding a knife to you. The threat is usually worse than the reality, more bark than bite. Most human dogs don't bite but their predator reflex gets pressed (encouraged) by another's weakness. Even if you are fabricating it, try to radiate confidence with your body. Lots of deep breaths through the nose, hold a few seconds then out through the mouth, shoulders back and trust in yourself.

The work of social psychologist Amy Cuddy has demonstrated that holding your body in a positive upright position with your legs planted shoulder-width apart can have a powerful effect on the brain. In her experiment, half the participants were asked to maintain weak body positions, shoulders hunched, sat down huddled over a phone with their arms crossed. The other half of the participants were asked to maintain strong physical positions, such as placing their hands on their hips like Batman, legs shoulder-width apart, head up, eyes wide, or legs planted and hands held up as if in victory. They were asked to hold these strong or weak positions for two minutes.

Immediately afterwards, each person was asked to

undergo a job interview. The interviewer had no idea of what had just happened to each person and simply judged them upon what took place in the meeting. Overwhelmingly, the result was that the people who maintained open and strong positions were deemed transparent, credible, trustworthy, engaged, energised and employable, while those who had been closed and weak in their body language were without exception considered by the interviewer to be untrustworthy, ambivalent, unenergised and lacking in confidence.

To back this up with hard science, Cuddy took saliva swabs from each person before and straight after they had held their position for two minutes. This revealed that those who'd held weaker positions produced greater levels of cortisol, the stress hormone associated with flight and fear – a staggering 19 per cent more than usual – while their strength hormone, testosterone, actually dipped by 25 per cent. Meanwhile, those who held strong positions were found to have experienced the opposite: their brains had told their bodies to be less fearful and more confident, and as a result, they produced 25 per cent less cortisol and 19 per cent more testosterone. This shows how my friend made his potential assailants feel he was more dangerous than he actually was just by squaring his shoulders and choosing to walk to them, rather than the other way round.

The brain has no idea that you are kidding it if you fake it with your body. Testosterone in excessive quantities results in 'red mist' (extreme, uncontrolled anger) or 'fight' in the fight or flight reaction. But testosterone in the right amounts means not only do you project strength to others, you also assert a self-belief in your body and in your mind. A quietly self-possessed person sits neither at the back nor front of the class – they don't need to stick their hand up or make themself heard as the class swot or clown; they are comfortable in their skin, a person you'd want watching your back in times of trouble. The moments in which they come alive and reveal this side are when they step in and help someone else in trouble or take the lead when they need to, not as a matter of course. For some reason, bullies and thugs seem to leave them alone and are wary of them. There's usually one in every class if you look for him or her. It's as if you could airdrop them anywhere in the world and they'd be fine. A confident smile goes a long way.

Judge your attacker

Your assailant could be high on drugs, drunk, a religious extremist, a gang member, someone with severe mental health problems, simply a bully or motivated by boredom. Depending on which you think they are, you need to decide whether there is a window to leave peacefully or whether you're going to have to fight to save your life. If they asked for your watch, hand it over – is a fancy watch really worth a hole in your lung or a blade in your kidney? Mental health is a major issue in many countries and there are people wandering the streets who would be much better off in a secure environment. These are the ones that you won't be able to reason with. In the same category you can add political or religious fundamentalists who are prepared to die for their extreme beliefs.

If your attempt at placating your assailant fails, consider running, but only if you know the terrain and where you're going to run to. Also bear in mind your level of fitness. If those two options are not feasible then you're going to have to cross your natural line of self-control and fight for your life. Here are a few suggestions:

Throat: Strike your attacker's throat with the heel of your hand, in one fluid motion. You need to be an arm's length away to be within striking distance. One hard hit to the Adam's apple will render them breathless and buy you some time to escape.

Crotch: Knee a male attacker in the crotch. You'll need to be close to do this. Better still, if you kick them in the testicles with your shin you can do so further away from the knife. Don't hold back, do it as hard as you can. If he drops the knife while doubled over, grab it and toss it as far as you can, then run.

Headbutt: If and only if their face is right opposite yours, surprise them with a headbutt, using the solid bone density of your forehead to smash the attacker on the nose.

Nose: Use the heel of your open hand and thrust it upward into the assailant's nose, aiming to hit the septum, the piece of bone between the nostrils.

Eyes: If the attacker is not interested in mugging you but trying to kill you then try to grab their wrist with one hand and use your first two fingers of the other hand to poke them in the eyes. Keep pushing the eyeballs and be prepared for a lot of blood.

Find a weapon to defend yourself with

There may not be much to hand in your immediate environment with which you can defend yourself. Look for a rock, lead pipe or plank of wood. Scan the area while keeping a close eye on the person. Let them lunge first and move back as they take a swipe at you, then hit them as hard as you can either on the wrist holding the knife or the head.

A top tip to remember here: whether the attacker is an animal or a knife-wielding maniac, remove your jacket and wrap it around your arm to take the bite or a strike as you unleash your wrath.

An attack from a bully

Bullies tend to have a pack with them to whom they show off their dominance by picking on safe bets - people they perceive as weaker than them. The psychology of the bully is based their own trauma; just as the abused often can become the abuser, the bullied becomes the bully. Part of them is broken and they can only feel better about what happened to them by revisiting something similar on someone else.

The best way to deal with a bully if your back is against

the wall is to take the fight to them, and so hard that they will never aggress you again. If you're ringed in by the bully's cronies and up close to the bully, you have to breathe deeply and do the unexpected. Go for the crotch with a snap kick and when they double over, twist your body as you throw an elbow punch to the nose. As your assailant goes down, make one more brutal hit to the back of his neck by making a fist – be sure to keep your thumb on the outside.

The common rule of thumb is that if you can fell your Grendel or Goliath, their minions will leave you alone and allow you to leave, for fear of receiving the same medicine themselves.

Bullies smell fear the way a shark smells blood in the water. Remember that whatever has happened between you and a bully, however much they have humiliated you in front of others and diminished your belief in yourself, even if you're down to your last scrap of self-respect, you *can* change the dynamic at any time. What matters is this moment right now, where if you choose to fight back you can change everything. Bullies seem to have an ability to sniff out other people's weaknesses; if they're a mental bully they often do this over a period of time in a way that's far more passive aggressive than the clear aggression of physical bullying, and therefore so much harder to deal with.

With physical bullies, fight back as if your life depends on it because it does; the trauma of being bullied will never leave you and that person, however far away you move from them, over however many years, will always seem to have a claim on you. So, get mad, get *really* mad, and give them a taste of their own medicine, even if it takes everything you've got – this one moment will positively flip your life. With mental bullies, play them at their own game: record them – without their knowing – being mean to you then play it to others like a teacher, your boss or a friend. Build your case against them with quiet satisfaction.

Extreme road rage

In the US in 2021, according to a poll conducted by an organisation called Everytown for Gun Safety, in 700 cases of road rage 500 people were shot, killed or wounded. It's a global problem and can range from tailgating, when somebody is driving behind you bumper-to-bumper, to drivers climbing out of their cars and trying to get into yours to harm you. The best thing you can do is not engage with the person angrily gesturing at you. Don't meet their eyes and remain calm. Stay in your vehicle and lock the doors. By engaging with the angered individual, you only open yourself up to things getting worse. The person is in red mist fight mode, they're hoping that you will meet their anger with a similar level of rage and they want to fight you.

To avoid road rage initially, try not to irritate other drivers or fly into anger when they irritate you. An AA (Automobile Association) poll of 18,000 of its members, revealed that a major frustration for motorists in the UK is when other drivers try to bully them with tailgating. Others are people talking on mobile phones, fast driving, drivers hogging the middle lane and undertaking from the inside. A lack of police presence on British motorways and roads doesn't help. Remember that the way in which you drive reflects how you're feeling, so when you're in a bad mood you are more likely to drive quicker and more impulsively, and more liable to get in an argument with another driver.

Rather than getting fixated on another bad driver, focus instead on the way you're driving. If you do accidentally cut someone up and they are clearly angry about it you can either put your hazards on so they blink twice, which is a way of saying 'thank you for letting me in' or 'sorry', or you can lower your window and put your hand up to say thank you. Most angry people will be placated by either of these gestures because it shows a willingness on your part to accept that you're in the wrong.

It's amazing how worked up people get within the confines of their car, especially in slow and gridlocked traffic. When you can't move your car and someone right next to you is staring at you with an angry expression, or worse, they're vocally threatening violence, is when you need to remain at your calmest. Some drivers are just looking to take a bad mood out on the first available person, so the best thing you can do is avoid eye contact with them and don't respond with any gestures that will inflame the situation further. So, no honking your horn or flashing your lights repeatedly.

If you are being tailgated or pressured by an impatient driver behind you, don't allow them to bully you into driving quicker. Remember to take deep breaths to remain balanced, as when we become stressed the first thing that we do is take short, shallow breaths, which starves our brain of oxygen and makes us more stressed. Don't stop the car in a layby just in case they decide to follow you but do slow down where the road allows so they are able to overtake. Alternatively, you can just drive round the first roundabout twice, allowing them to go ahead of you.

The AA advises that if you are being consistently followed by an angry driver who just won't let it go, your best bet is to drive to a police station. If you can't find one, then head to a public place with plenty of people. A fuel garage is a good place to stop as there are plenty of CCTV cameras in plain view, or a busy street. From here, you can call the police and hopefully the presence of lots of witnesses will be sufficient deterrent to make the driver check himself and drive off. If you have somebody with you in the passenger seat, they could video the other driver just to make them think twice about taking it any further. If you are stopped and an angry driver stops behind you, don't get out of the car, even to want to try and reason with them or apologise; the chances are this will be a red rag to a bull and they will have a very different agenda.

Another word of caution on the subject of a driver who's been following behind you for what seems an unnaturally long time: however tempting it might be, don't drive home.

The last thing you want is some nutter knowing where you live. It's interesting that levels of road rage went right down during the pandemic. Of course, many of us were in lockdown and so we weren't using our cars much, but even when we did drive, we weren't commuting to work or following a tight schedule in which we blamed others for making us late. With the current difficult economic circumstances, road rage figures have shot back up again to reflect this stress.

Carjacking

Carjacking is the theft of a car from its driver by force or intimidation. Common carjacking ruses include 'bump and rob', whereby the thief softly rear-ends the victim's vehicle at traffic lights and when they get out of their vehicle to assess the damage and exchange insurance information, a second carjacker nips in and drives their car away. Another is the 'good samaritan', in which the attacker(s) stage what looks to have been an accident and feigns injury, and when a driver stops, they are forced out of their car at gunpoint, while another drives their car away. The 'ruse' involves the car behind you flashing their lights and waving as if there is something wrong with your car. You pull over, they nab your car.

Between 2019 and 2021, London saw 2,663 incidents of carjacking. In the US there are over 34,000 carjacking incidents per year, 90 per cent of which take place in cities or suburbs.

What to do if you are threatened by a carjacker

Avoiding confrontation is the best approach. If there's a gun pointed at your head, however angry it might make you don't thwart the criminal but let them go about their business. This may seem cowardly, but, let's be honest, if someone has a gun, it's not worth the risk. This is what you pay insurance for. Instead:

- If you've been bumped from behind, consider where you stop. If it's somewhere where there are no people, motion to the driver behind to follow you and put your hazard lights on. Only get out of the car in a public place with people or in a garage in full view of CCTV and the staff.
- Think before stopping to help in an accident; it may be safer to call and report it to the police.
- Assess if stopped cars are damaged or not before climbing out of the car and being a good samaritan. They may be blocking the road, so if you are sure something feels off, be prepared to drive through the blockade.
- Try to note the characteristics of the person who wants you to stop – their build, hair and eye colour and complexion. Also, mentally photograph their car, noting the numberplate, colour.
- If you find yourself in a carjacking situation, try to remain calm, don't escalate the situation. Attackers usually want your car, not your life.

Nor do they want your kids – always negotiate their safe exit from the vehicle before you get out and hand over the keys.

- If you're on your own, look for an escape route once you leave the vehicle.
- Hand over your keys.

Mass shooting

According to the FBI, between 2000 and 2019, 2,851 people died in 333 mass shootings in the US, the majority of which were carried out by lone gunmen with average age of 18. No place it seems is exempt, even the sanctity of a church. When it comes to attacks on schools, there is usually a connection between the shooter and the school; they are either current students or alumni. For the shooter this is usually the final act, the endgame which is capped off by them taking their own life. It's not just school children who are at risk of mass shootings, grocery stores in the US are also targeted. For example, on 14 May 2022, a racially motivated attack was carried out on Black shoppers in an African-American neighbourhood, resulting in ten people losing their lives.

In the US, tragedies like this have been growing in frequency. Criminologists believe there's a pattern to mass shootings, with one usually sparking a glut of others. According to the Violence Project, who conducted the largest study of mass shootings ever funded by the US government, 'One mass shooting happens and then you see a few happen right after that.' Their data on shootings across America reveals there is a two-week window following the initial shooting during which there's a lot of media attention, which gives others the idea to launch their own hate shooting.

What to do if you are caught in a mass shooting

Already knowing where the exits are is key information in the event of a lone gunman entering a school, church or workplace. The likelihood of anything happening is small but never say never. Similarly, if you live in the US and you shop at the mall, make a mental map of where the exit points are.

The US Department of Homeland Security suggests using the 'run, hide, fight' model if you ever find yourself in a mass shooting:

Run: Experts on counter terrorism suggest that you have a better chance of survival if you try to flee the scene of an active shooter, rather than lying on the ground, holding your breath and playing dead. But don't run blindly in any direction; listen to where the gunshots are coming from to try to figure out the gunman's location, then plan your own escape accordingly. The first ten seconds of a shooting are key to your survival; you can either get yourself out of the kill zone or get stuck in it. If you hear the discharge of an assault rifle it will be very noisy and presumably like nothing you've heard before. You need to move quietly and quickly, drawing as little attention to yourself as possible. Try to keep a little distance between you and any wall next to you as bullets may ricochet and strike you.

Hide: If it's not possible to get clear of the kill zone you need to find points of cover where you are shielded from bullets and concealed points where you cannot be seen. Move from one point to the other until you find safety. Useful external cover includes cars, cement blocks and walls. Internal cover might include filing cabinets but avoid hiding under a desk as this is an obvious place. If you can, find a storeroom with a key, lock yourself in and hide behind rows of furniture. Though only do this if the door opens into the room and you can barricade yourself in - it's pointless if the door opens outwards. Remember to turn off the lights so you won't catch the killer's attention. The average time of a mass shooting is about 15 minutes. After this point, police snipers will hopefully be in position ready to take down the shooter, so every moment that you can stay hidden is a win.

Fight: This is the absolute last resort, when you have no choice but to fight for your life. Never attempt this on your own. Coordinate your attack on the gunman with others, nominating one person to distract them and draw their attention away from the people who will rush the gunman and overpower him. Waiting for the for the right moment is essential. Every moment that you're alive the rescue team is getting closer. Be patient and wait till the gunman is reloading in those precious few seconds if there's enough of you who might be able to overpower him. Find a weapon, anything that can disable him. And show no mercy.

The closer you are to the gunman, the better. One of you should try to disarm him while the other takes his legs out. An elbow used to strike at the face is a lot harder than a fist and won't hurt you in your delivery of it. It should be executed as if you are throwing a boxing hook. If you have scissors or a pen you can try to stab the shooter's eyes, face and neck, while someone else slams down on his arms with anything heavy so your assailant will hopefully release their firearm. If your shooter is male, which is frequently the case, then kick them as hard as you can in the crotch. Whatever you do, don't try to negotiate with the shooter; they know how they want it to end and it certainly isn't going to make any difference if you're pleading for your life.

TERRORIST ATTACK

Suicide bombers and machete-wielding Muslim extremists have become a tragic thorn in the side of Western societies and a stain on the gentle, peace-affirming faith of Islam.

The bloodshed caused by a suicide bomber is appalling. In some cases, how you react in a situation determines whether you live to see another day as there are certain things that you can do which give you a better chance of survival. First, vigilance is key. In order to maximise the carnage they inflict, terrorist attacks always happen in crowded areas. If there's anything that triggers your instinct, then tell a police officer or call a confidential police antiterrorism hotline. Any piece of information, however small, could be really important so it's better to be safe and report something if it doesn't feel right to you. That feeling you get in your gut may be responsible for saving scores of lives.

Public transport and iconic locations where crowds of tourists gather have been targets for terrorists in the past. Look out for people in stationary vehicles watching a building and looking shifty, or vehicles which keep driving slowly near public buildings as if they're casing them out; maybe it's an individual making notes or taking pictures of an entry and exit point in a building. If you feel uncomfortable in the situation, leave. Remember that there are as many neurons in your gut as a cat has in its brain, so these hunches are often correct even if you can't place exactly what is going on – it's a feeling you get.

If you hear gunfire, try to establish where it came from and head in the opposite direction. If you're in a building located close to the site of a terrorist attack, stay away from the windows. And if you are in the vicinity of an attack, don't stay around to watch what happens; there may be additional extremists involved and there may be more than one stage of the attack. Stay clear of glass shopfronts and if there's a crowd, get away from it as quickly as possible in case another suicide bomber's operating.

In Afghanistan, one Taliban tactic was to trigger an IED (improvised explosive device) and then just when the Allied forces arrived, another device, or suicide bomber, would activate their explosive belt to create a second wave of carnage. If you find yourself inside a building in a bomb-threat scenario, stay away from the windows because they can shatter with the force of an explosion, which may also push you out of the window. In the event of a bomb detonating, the best place to be is under a desk where you have some protection from falling debris.

After the attack, seek professional help if needed. Dramatic events can have a long-lasting impact on mental health and it's important to seek support if, months after the event, it's still haunting you.

KIDNAPPING

Someone may be kidnapped for a ransom, to force them to withdraw money from an ATM, to subject them to some form of involuntary servitude or sexual assault, to take them away from the other parent or for political purposes. Of all the different kinds of kidnap, the most disturbing is that which is perpetrated against children.

Child abduction

How common are child abductions? According to the charity Action Against Abduction, 'roughly 50 children under the age of 16 are abducted by strangers every year' in the UK, while the NSPCC estimates that, 'In the UK, one in every 100 children faces an abduction attempt at some point in their childhood or teenage years. However, this figure is heavily biased towards single-parent homes and families on a low income.'

Forty-two per cent of all abduction attempts are made by strangers and 75 per cent of these are unsuccessful. The average age of abducted children is 13.

The most common form of non-sexual child kidnapping is the abduction of a child by a desperate parent locked in a bitter custody rivalry. This is sometimes called 'family kidnapping' as it usually involves the child being kept hidden by a family member on behalf of the kidnapping parent. Often these cases are resolved when the offending parent comes to their senses and realises the well-being of the child is more important than winning a battle with their spouse.

In some scenarios, the husband or wife, partner or ex, will take their child abroad with them without permission from the other parent. The most frequent destination countries for children abducted from the UK are Kuwait, Poland, Spain, India, the US, Pakistan, Romania and Germany. In the event that it happens to your child, you should immediately contact the police, who will ask you the following:

- A description of your child and their full name
- Why they have been abducted

- When they were taken
- Who may have taken your child
- Where you think your child might be now
- Where the child might be taken in the future
- Vehicle details of the person who may have taken your child.
- Details of any previous threats to take your child and any previous abductions or attempted abductions
- Whether your child has their own passport and where the passport was issued
- Their passport number, whether your child has dual nationality and more than one passport
- If you have your child's birth certificate
- Any agreements or court orders which apply to the child.

If your child has not already been taken abroad the police will issue a 'port alert', whereby the National Border Targeting Centre will alert all points of departure (ports and airports) to prevent your child from being taken out of the country. The port alert can last a maximum of 28 days. If you're worried about the well-being and safety of your child, police can issue a CRA (child rescue alert), which then seeks to involve the press and the public to ensure that there are more on the lookout.

Ollie Experience: Kidnapped

When I was working as a security contractor and country manager in post-war Iraq, managing an army of 2,000 local Iraqi soldiers, there was a lot of kidnapping of local employees who worked for Western companies. Their presence proved vital while the power grid was repaired and new mobile phone networks were installed. One of our employees was taken. A colleague of mine spoke to the kidnappers and in the background he could hear someone having his head cut off. After we paid the ransom his captors killed him anyway. You need to get regular proof of life when you're negotiating. Also, the longer you leave the person with the kidnappers, the thinner your chances are of getting them back alive.

How to talk to your children about the possibility of abduction

In the UK in the early 1970s, there was a government awareness campaign called 'stranger danger'. The focus was purely on looking out for strangers who might abduct kids – which put the fear of God into many who were children at the time – but now we know that, statistically speaking, a child is more likely to be abducted by somebody they know. Only warning children about strangers gives them a false sense of security around familiar adults.

Children are generally encouraged to do as adults ask, so we need to find an age-appropriate way to ensure they feel empowered to look out for their own safety. One way is to implement a 'check first' safety rule. This is where you teach your children that *any* time anyone is trying to get them to go somewhere, even when it's someone they know and are comfortable with, they must first check with the parent or adult in charge. It's important to stress to your kids that if somebody breaks the check first safety rule, they can come and tell you and you won't be angry or disappointed and they won't be in trouble. If it feels wrong to them, it probably is. If an adult doesn't respect their check first rule and tries to override it to get them in a car, children should scream at the top of their voice, making it clear that they're not playing by yelling something specific like, 'Call the police!' or 'Stay away from me!'

It's important that kids know they should never have any reason to keep a secret from their parents or guardian and that they can come to you with any problem. This open line of communication with you will protect them from grooming predators who tell them to keep secrets in return for gifts, sweets, money or other temptations. When children know that secrets are not healthy, if that happens, they are far more likely to come and tell you immediately.

Most abductions of children occur between 2pm and 7pm when a child may be out riding their bike or walking alone from school or a friend's house. Parents should encourage their kids to always be with a friend whenever they're away from home; just increasing the number by one drastically reduces the chance of abduction.

Express kidnapping

The likelihood of you being kidnapped is very slim, but you are more at risk in the developing world. The Philippines is currently the most likely place to be kidnapped. However, the target is usually wealthy Chinese businessmen. A more likely scenario in developing countries is the express kidnapping, when somebody appears while you are using an ATM and forces you into their vehicle at gunpoint, then drives to different ATMs, forcing you to get out as much money as you can. These kidnappers are low-grade criminals and are most probably inexperienced and jumpy. They may be high or drunk, so assess carefully whether you think you can take them down or not. If they have a gun pointed at you and you're in the middle of nowhere it's not worth screaming or shouting and it may be easier to comply. In cases of express kidnapping, the victim is usually let go after they've got the cash. They don't need to keep you any longer nor do they want to draw attention to themselves by hurting a tourist. Many poor countries rely on the income of the tourist dollar and come down hard on local criminals who endanger this.

Latin America and Africa, because of the depths of poverty there, are places where you can expect kidnapping of this nature and tourists who, sadly, are not aware of this are easy pickings. You can avoid this happening by applying some common sense. If you're on the wrong side of the city and down a dark street, you're making yourself an easy target because you're in the backyard of these petty criminals. Look for an ATM in an area which is well lit, preferably with a security door. Always look behind you to check that you're not being watched and if somebody appears and gets uncomfortably close to you, ask them to back off or cancel the withdrawal and wait for them to leave.

Be careful of an over-friendly stranger who seems to hone in on you in a bar or tourist area and offers to take you for a drink as it could well be a prelude to a kidnapping. Weary travellers arriving in a strange place at night are extremely vulnerable, so don't hang around; if you're an independent traveller, head to your guesthouse as soon as possible. Things look different in the sunlight and once you've become a little more aware of your surroundings you can relax a bit, but always keep a secret stash of money and a credit card separately from your wallet in the event that the latter is taken. Do your homework on the places you go to; look for reviews where other travellers have shared their experience. As a general rule, bus and train stations tend to attract opportunistic thieves.

Kidnap for extortion

The offspring of very wealthy parents and high-profile figures like actors can be targeted by kidnappers hoping to gain a hefty ransom. The British, Australian and US governments have a policy of not negotiating with kidnap demands, while France and Italy do. The British Counterterrorism and Security Bill states, 'Terrorists have long used kidnap for ransom to raise money to increase their capability. Payment of terrorist ransoms not only strengthens terrorists' ability to organise and carry out terrorist attacks; it also enables them to maintain their groups, recruit and retain members – and it incentivises future kidnaps. Terrorist groups operating in Syria and Iraq – including ISIL – are using kidnap for ransom to raise funds.'

In the case of carefully targeted kidnappings, your kidnappers are very different beasts from the low-level opportunist at an ATM. They are highly skilled planners, sometimes ex-military, with a chain of contacts in the criminal underworld.

What to do if someone tries to kidnap you

The best time to resist an attempted kidnapping is in the first few seconds of it happening. It's also the most dangerous for the kidnapper(s) because they may have to nab you in broad daylight in a built-up area and risk being identified. This is when you have your strongest chance to escape. Make a lot of noise to attract people's attention. Scream 'Police!' at the top of your lungs, or 'Help me!' The more people that witness your abduction (if it is successful), the greater chance at least a few of them will call the police and be able to provide a physical description of your abductor(s) and/or the vehicle make, colour and registration number.

Most kidnap attempts which are unsuccessful are due to the victim fighting back. Generally, victims are too scared and shocked to resist, so when you do something unexpected like headbutt or kick your assailant in the groin, you win yourself some precious time. Throw everything you've got into attacking them and by no means be squeamish, get angry! Look for an object in your immediate environment that you can hit them with. Go for the soft bits of their anatomy like the eyes, throat and testicles. Whatever happens, don't let them get you in a car as it will be much harder for the authorities to find you if your attacker drives you a long distance. Once you're inside the confines of a moving vehicle your captor has the control, your chances of escaping are more than halved and you might not have another opportunity to run. If you do manage to get away from their grasp, head for somewhere which is well lit (if it's dark) and where there will be plenty of people.

Escaping from the boot of a kidnapper's car

You may be subdued with a handkerchief soaked in chloroform to stop you resisting, which will immediately put you to sleep. But if you're put into a vehicle while you're conscious, try to pay as much attention as possible to the trip your captor is taking, like how long the car travels without stopping, the direction of any turns or any sounds you notice on the road. If you're lucky you may still have your phone on you and can call the police. Give them as much accurate information as you can about the car you're in, your current location and what happened leading up to the situation. The good news is that the police can track your phone.

Cars manufactured after 2002 are required to have a boot release cord in the boot, thanks to a law in the UK brought in to protect children from getting locked in and dying of CO2 poisoning. If you're lucky enough to be in one of these cars and your abductor was dumb enough to overlook it, find the release and pull or press it. Even if you're trapped in a car manufactured before 2002, most have a jack stored in the boot, which you might be able to get at. Position the contraption close to the boot latch and repeatedly turn the handle on the jack until it forces the door open. It also gives you a weapon to surprise and incapacitate your captor with.

If this isn't possible you can try to kick out the brake lights by peeling back the carpet on the rear sides of the car and feeling where the lights are. If you can smash through the plastic lens and casing and remove the brake light unit, you should be able to look through the open cavity and take in your surroundings. Choose your time carefully, like when there is another car directly behind, then put your arm through and start waving frantically. It would be even better if you can first write 'HELP!' on your palm. Time is crucial because the likelihood is your kidnappers are taking you somewhere remote and unpopulated so you can't easily be found.

In the event no cars are following you, don't lose this precious observation time in panic but take in as much of the environment you're passing through as possible, as it could eventually be your escape route. While you're in transit, listen out for different voices in the car. If there's only one person, there is a chance they may stop at some point in the journey. If you hear them getting out of the car, try to push through the back seat if it folds down.

What to do once you are in captivity

If your initial attempts at resistance have foundered, your strategy must change immediately. You now have to be as docile and agreeable as you can make yourself. Avoid eye contact initially; you need to convince your jailers that you are not a threat and give them a false sense of security so they make mistakes. Start evaluating your surroundings, looking for possible exits, and try to get an understanding of the layout of their hide. Consider their state of mind – are they calm or desperate and edgy? Why have they taken you? Try to find out their motivation – is it money, revenge or political?

If you're a ransom target or being trafficked by a people-smuggling gang, there's every chance that you will be moved to different locations multiple times. Your kidnappers may not feed you well, in which case you will feel yourself getting weaker, your body lacking the vital energy it needs if you're going to try to escape and your mind blurry at a time when it needs to be sharp. Keeping your survival mindset going will get harder and harder as time progresses.

Begin to build a relationship with your captors by politely asking for a drink, a blanket, some food, etc., reminding them that you're not a slab of meat with a dollar sign on it, you're a human being like them and need the same things that they do. Avoid any inflammable subjects of conversation like religion. Gradually, try to find a link between them and you – maybe you've both got a son, perhaps there's an important football match coming up in which you could share a common interest. Tell them your name, tell them about your kids and how much you love to be a parent, describe your children in detail, what you love doing with them, when their birthdays are . . . Rapport builds trust and empathy. If you can highlight that you have a shared interest, subconsciously your captor will feel you are less of a threat because you are like them. If you have some pictures of your family, show them to your kidnapper. Tell them about yourself, where you were born, how you met your partner, where you were supposed to be this week if you hadn't been kidnapped. By building a fuller picture of yourself you're appealing to everything that's human about them and making it more difficult for them to inflict pain on you or even kill you.

Provided your captors are calm and feed you daily there's a good chance you'll make it out alive. Privately, try to create your own routine. It will give you a sense of autonomy in a situation where there is very little you can control. Exercising and meditating will help to maintain strength and mental fitness. Try to keep a handle on the time and date by observing the light in your cell, temperature and sounds of animals whose schedule you will quickly become familiar with. Think of your family often and how you will see them again, plan a trip abroad somewhere with them – imagine it, smell the warm sand, taste the mojito – to give yourself something to keep you going forward.

If you're lucky, there will be a rescue attempt. This is the second most dangerous moment in your ordeal (after your first capture) because you may be used by your kidnappers as a human shield. Your rescue team will be packing heavy firepower and though they will have seen a photo of you in their briefing, you might now have a beard or depending on how long you've been held captive, you may have aged. Lie down on the ground and cover your head.

If your captors' manner towards you becomes remote and they stop feeding you, it's likely that the negotiators failed, the ransom wasn't paid and your captors are about to kill you. If you're lucky you may have a few hours and this is the time you must take the risk of attempting escape; at least if you die it will be while you are in control of your existence.

WILD ANIMAL ATTACKS

Bear attacks

Bear populations are spread all over the world, from Vietnam to the Arctic, from the Mongolian steppe to

Romania. If you happen to encounter a bear not armed with marmalade sandwiches, the following rhyme is worth remembering: 'If it's black, fight back. If it's brown, lay down. If it's white, good night.' The largest number of attacks on humans come from grizzlies, because their habitat in so many areas is shared with or encroached on by humans, whereas polar bears live in a region seldom visited by us. With urban areas constantly demanding more space for larger populations and suburbs expanding into the habitat of wildlife, conflicts between humans and bears will happen. The more we trespass into wilder territory, the greater the increased threat to our pets, too, many of which will be easy pickings for big wildlife. And because hunting their prey has become more competitive in a smaller area due to human incursions, wild omnivores like bears are forced to go through bins and feed on domestic animals.

European brown bears

A little smaller than their grizzly cousins, European brown bears are still huge and found in their highest density in Romania. The reason the country has such an abundance of brown bear (and wolf and lynx) is because for years their former dictator, Nicolae Ceausescu, forbade anyone hunting in the country's huge Carpathian forests apart from him – the penalty was no salary for a whole year. As such there are now more (around 7,000) brown bears than anywhere else in Europe, and not surprisingly, this is where most of the attacks in occur. The human-animal conflict is acute in the city of Brasov, known as the gateway to Transylvania, where brown bears are drawn to the municipal rubbish dump, where they have easy food, not to mention the odd drunk in the park who goes missing after sleeping on a park bench at night.

Polar bears

The polar bear is classed as a marine animal because of the time it spends in the water. With serious stamina, this powerhouse of a carnivore can swim for two days without rest. The species is widely distributed throughout the Arctic region and is the largest carnivore on the planet (on its hind legs, it can stand up to three metres tall). Possessing a formidable sense of smell, a polar bear can sniff you from a staggering 32 kilometres away and will hunt you down with determination. Because climate change is thinning pack ice where traditionally the polar bear finds its prey, it is having to venture vast distances into the realm of humans to eat.

By nature, the polar bear is curious and investigative. Avoid travelling in their habitat at night, even by car. Ensure you have bear spray (see also page 224) and a gun if you're out on foot. If you're camping, don't attract unwanted attention by leaving your food boxes open or your stash close to your tent; always keep it in airtight containers. Never sleep without perimeter security (electric fencing) around your camp. Bears are usually found close to the shoreline so move inland to set up camp. Try to avoid cooking in the place you sleep.

Attacks on humans are almost always carried out by young, malnourished male bears and the majority of these are on lone individuals or very small groups of people. If you see a polar bear and it hasn't seen you, freeze and hope this continues until it wanders off, then back slowly away. If it charges, you need to react very quickly. Never run from a polar bear. Unlike grizzlies, it won't mock charge you. The best defence is a gun. If you have a firearm, fire off a warning round where possible and that should be sufficient to send the bear on its way. However, if it's not, aim straight for the head, under the chin. Because not many of us are used to the sight of a lumbering killing machine rapidly closing in on us, guns have only a 76 per cent success rate in stopping a bear.

New scientific findings (funded by Polar Bears International) reveal that bear spray is 98 per cent effective with a range of up to four metres, but you need to have balls of steel to wait until the animal gets so close that you can spray it. It also needs to be downwind of you otherwise the pepper spray will go in your eyes. A bear's life depends on its ability to see and smell prey, so if all you have is a knife, attack its nose and eyes. Signal flares are also useful deterrents as the light is similar to fire, which even polar bears are afraid of. Few attacked by these massive beasts have lived to tell the tale though.

Case Study: Faulty kit leads to tragic death on Svalbard

There are more polar bears in Arctic Norway's Svalbard Island than anywhere else on Earth. In 2011, some 80 British students were on an expedition to Svalbard organised by the British Schools Exploring Society (BSES). Human beings are very much on the menu of the world's largest bear, but parents of the children had been assured that the expedition campsite where they slept would be rigged with tripwires that set off small explosive flares. They were also told that one of the teachers would have a firearm in case of emergency. However, while the students slept, a starving male bear was able to enter the camp as the tripwire mines weren't working. It attacked two boys in a tent, biting one in the head and then savaging another boy, 17-year-old Horatio Chapple, to death. The so-called firearm was an old rifle that the teacher was unable to operate.

Grizzly bears

Grizzlies are a sub species of brown bear found across Canada and North America and are responsible for most fatal and non-fatal attacks on humans. The attacks usually come from injured and therefore famished male grizzlies, sub-adult males or acutely protective female grizzlies who feel there's a threat to their cub - so *never* walk between a mother and her young. Males are larger than females and stand two or three metres on their hind legs.

They have a terrific sense of smell, seven times stronger than a bloodhound, and though humans are not on their menu, if you surprise them then they are likely to attack or run away. There's a good chance they'll leave you alone if they've already eaten and you make sufficient noise so they can hear you coming.

When looking for somewhere to camp, keep your eye out for bear tracks and for their scat (poo), as this means they've been in the vicinity. If the scat is still soft and warm, the bear will be close so you need to make some noise. Grizzly scat varies in colour depending on what the bear has been eating; remember they're omnivores so they survive not just on meat but berries and grass as well. You're basically looking for a huge pile of shit that might be purple, black and full of berries, green with bits of grass or black with animal hair in it.

Another giveaway of their presence is a nest where they have laid down for a snooze, often at the side of a bear track. The grass will be flattened in a circle. As apex predators they will happily wander into a human camp without fear if they smell food. Every year somebody is killed by a grizzly because they've neglected to keep their food separate from where they sleep at night. Ensure all food containers are sealed airtight, or hang them high up in a tree, and this includes chocolate or energy bars.

A 1994 study by the International Association for Bear Research and Management revealed that 61 per cent of hikers attacked by grizzlies in Yellowstone Park tried to run away or climb a tree. Neither is a good option; when you run from a predator that's you saying you're scared and it triggers their 'pursuit instinct'. Also, grizzlies can run at 35mph for extended periods (and just like polar bears, they can outswim you too). While a fully grown male cannot shin up a tree because their body mass is too much for their legs to support and their claws are curled inwards, sub-adult grizzlies are lighter and can.

Remember the earlier poem: 'If it's brown, lay down'. Although it might seem counterintuitive, fighting your urge to run, lying face down on the ground with your knees tucked under your chin and covering the back of your head with your hands and keeping still – as if to play dead – is the best you can do. By making yourself smaller you become less of a threat to the bear. At best, it will lose interest after biting you a few times or stamping on you with its forepaws and then move on.

If it thinks you're alive it will maul you and this is when your only option is to fight back. Always go for the eyes with your knife. Unlike predators such as big cats who bite the neck of their prey and choke it to death, or bite through the skull causing instant death before settling down to eat, grizzly bears are happy to take their time devouring you while you are you still alive, ripping off an arm to chew on or tearing off a buttock. They will leave you, have a nap and then return for another feed.

Grizzlies hate the smell of mothballs, so take plenty of these to scatter around your tent. The other deterrent is to use pepper spray when the animal is around nine metres away, but only if the bear is downwind of you. Spray towards the ground as the bear will have its head down as it charges you. One final suggestion is to make yourself seem much bigger, but this approach is only possible if the animal is trailing you at a distance. Use two x three-metre branches to form a huge cross, tying the two pieces together securely with your belt, and drape an open sleeping bag, rug, binbag or bivvy bag over the structure (like wings), placing yourself in front of it, so from a distance you look to be one animal. Then make a hell of a lot of noise.

Case Study: Grizzly Man

Few documentaries pack the tragic punch of *Grizzly Man*, the story of an ex-actor-turned-bear-whisperer and conservationist, Timothy Treadwell. Every summer for 13 years, Treadwell would leave California and head to the wilds of Alaska, where he would catch a ride in a float plane to Katmai National Park & Preserve, which is home to around 3,000 bears, about 10 per cent of the world's grizzly population, to spend his summer living among wild grizzlies. He soon became famous for his outrageously brave (some would say naïve) selfie videos in which he would be so close to the bears that he could almost touch them. He got to recognise each one of them individually, giving them a name, and seemed to know how far he could push it with each. Treadwell had an endearingly childish innocence about him and he trusted the bears with his life. He didn't even carry pepper spray, never mind a gun. Incredibly, the bears tolerated him, even the mothers with cubs seemed to know he wasn't a threat.

Although Treadwell often fell foul of the Katmai National Park rangers, with violations including improper storage of food, wildlife harassment, use of a portable generator and guiding tourists without a licence, there was one rule he never flouted and that was to leave when the grizzlies went to their dens to hibernate at the end of September. The only bears who didn't go to ground then would be older or injured bears who had not been strong enough to feed up adequately for the big sleep and were still roaming about hungry. Treadwell observed his rule but then following an argument with a stranger back in Anchorage and civilisation, he asked his friend and float plane pilot Willy Fulton to take him back for one more week in the wilderness.

Treadwell and his girlfriend Amie Huguenard were eaten alive by a mean-looking bear he was unfamiliar with. The conservationist left the sound on his video recorder and it captured their deaths when the bear attacked. As scheduled, at 2pm on Monday 6 October 2003, Willie Fulton arrived at Kaflia Lake to pick them up and was approached by a big grizzly. No one answered his calls and as he repeatedly flew over the campsite to scare the bear away, he spotted it with its head in his dead friend's ribcage. Three rangers later fired at the bear; it took them 21 shots to kill it. The six-minute audio recording of Timothy and Amie's harrowing deaths has never been released.

Black bears

With an estimated population of 900,000 in North America and Canada, you're more likely to meet a black bear than any other bear in these ranges. Smaller and less aggressive than a grizzly or polar bear, black bears are non-predatory omnivores, but though they generally prefer to flee in the presence of humans, they are still responsible for attacks and occasional fatalities (less than one per year). Confusingly, black bears are not only black; in fact, they come in many colours, from cinnamon to caramel and brown. To clearly distinguish a brown-coloured black bear from a grizzly, look to see if it has the grizzly's telltale huge hump of muscle between its shoulders and rounded ears.

There have been 25 human fatalities due to black bears in the last 20 years. A Journal of Wildlife Management study of black bear aggression found that 92 per cent of fatal black bear attacks were carried out by lone males and occurred in the month of August, a favourite time for hikers, when the bears are fattening up in preparation to hibernate. Every year, there are millions of human interactions with black bears that pass without incident, but remember, a black bear can run, swim and climb quicker than we can and if one wants to kill you, it has the hardware to do so. If you see a bear, pick up small kids and dogs immediately, then make plenty of noise to alert it to your presence.

'If it's black, fight back.' But before resorting to this, first make yourself look bigger and shout and wave your arms. Always stand your ground, never turn around and run, and never play dead. If you have pepper spray, use it when the bear is still 12 metres away. If not, kick the animal in the face and nose.

Puma attacks

Also known as a mountain lion, catamount or cougar, these large predators are widely spread across the US (from Montana down to Florida) and Canada but can be found as far afield as Chile. As a rule, pumas eat prey smaller than themselves. Of the 27 known human fatalities due to puma attacks, almost half were kids under 13. Pumas hunt at dusk and dawn and are sometimes drawn to lone cyclists and runners in national parks because their movement triggers the animal's pursuit instinct. These are usually ambushes that you won't see coming.

If you do spot a puma, make eye contact with it. Be sure to look confident and talk calmly and loudly, then gradually back away. Never take your eye off a puma, not even for a second – by turning your back, you are suggesting that you are afraid, and their favourite method of killing is by attacking the spinal cord. Incredibly agile, it's said that these cats can jump 4.5 metres vertically and 12 metres from standing – which means that if it decides to attack, a puma can close the space between the two of you very quickly.

Make yourself look bigger and throw something at it, but never crouch down to pick something up as this is yet another signal that will encourage it to attack you. As far as the puma is concerned, you just got smaller and therefore easier to kill. Your chances of surviving an attack one-on-one are pretty good; go for the animal's eyes, smash it on the nose and most likely, it will leave you alone. Pepper spray is also effective.

Case Study: Living to tell the tale

Anne Hjelle, a 48-year-old from Orange County, California, and her friend Debbie were cycling on a trail near Whiting Ranch in Orange County when they met a man who said he'd found an abandoned bike and was looking for its owner. They carried on cycling and as they were going downhill towards a ravine, something reddish-yellow in colour appeared in Hjelle's peripheral vision from the scrub. At first, she thought it was a deer but the sheer weight of it as it dug its claws into her back, slamming her onto the ground, was phenomenal. It was a huge mountain lion.

Taking Hjelle by the scruff of her neck in its jaws,

it began to drag her down to the ravine. She managed to punch the big cat in the face a few times, but to no avail. Her friend Debbie had hold of her leg and was in a tug-of-war with the cougar, who now had Hjelle's head clamped in its jaws. Next, it tore off her cheek and Hjelle was ready to die as her vision went black. When she woke up, the cat was gone, thanks to the arrival of a few other cyclists, who threw rocks at the animal, one of which hit it squarely on the head; it released its prey and made off into the bush. Hjelle was now choking on her own blood and the left side of her face she remembers was as if 'somebody had stapled a steak to it'.

As the medical emergency helicopter arrived, the pilot could see the cat crouched at the near distance to the survivor and the other cyclists; it hadn't given up and was waiting for another chance. Later, the local sheriff's

department found a body which was identified as the owner of the abandoned bike, Mark Reynolds. Reynolds was an athlete but he was also a lone figure, which made him a more tempting target for the cat. Hjelle reckons she wouldn't have survived had she been on her own and it was only thanks to her friend, and the cyclists who joined the fight, that she kept her life. That and a little luck – of the 20 deep wounds she sustained during the attack, none of them punctured her trachea, oesophagus or voice box, or connected with her carotid arteries, which doctors thought was nothing short of a miracle.

Wolf attacks

Wolves are enjoying a comeback, especially in Europe, where you'll find most of them in the forests of Romania. Grey wolves and timber wolves can be found in Alaska and Canada. Wolfpacks usually number between ten and 12 individuals. Every pack has an alpha female and male and they're the only ones who are allowed to mate. Your likelihood of bumping into a wolf is almost zero, given that wolves are naturally wary of humans and that their hearing is 16 times stronger than ours; you might find their scat (poo) but the animal itself will have disappeared like a ghost.

However, if you do come face-to-face with a wolf the best thing you can do to calm the situation is by avoiding eye contact, as they'll consider this a challenge. If you lower your head and bow slightly, this will be interpreted as submissive behaviour. You should then back away very slowly, but never turn your back on a wolf. If it's a lone wolf snarling at you and gradually advancing, things are escalating in the wrong direction; you now need to stare at it, making yourself look as large and aggressive as possible, while shouting, clapping and making as much noise as you can. Use anything to hand to fight with if it starts to attack.

A wolf's olfactory brilliance (sense of smell) is key to its survival so go for the nose or the eyes. One thing wolves hate is fire – if you grab a burning stick and wave it at them, this will keep them at bay. If it's a pack you find yourself up against, all you can do is climb a tree and hope that they will go away after smelling a more tasty dinner. Never let wolves get behind you or run from them, as both actions will trigger their prey drive to kick in.

Ollie Experience: Fish bait meets *The Hangover*
Flying back from a military operation in Malaysia, we stopped halfway somewhere in the Middle East for the night. It became an unofficial night out and a great chance to and let our hair down. The carnage the next morning was like a scene from the film *The Hangover*, only worse . . . With aching heads and woozy vision, we all compared what we could remember of the previous night, and then somebody said, 'Did you hear about Eddy? He's had his finger bitten off by a tiger.' It seemed him and a few others had drunkenly broken into a zoo and, mistaking the resident Bengal tiger for a harmless moggy, Eddy had climbed in its cage and tried to stroke it, whereupon it bit off his finger. He turned up with a huge bandage on his hand. A welcome reminder to us all that it pays to watch your alcohol intake and to avoid trying to stroke a tiger!

Crocodile and alligator attacks

Whether its deepest Borneo or the swamps of Floridian Alligator Alley, the Amazon basin or the savannah of Botswana, you'll find crocs and alligators all over the world (they live on five different continents). Of the two, crocodiles are much more aggressive and likely to go for you, but a hungry alligator who spots an easy lunch will happily eat you. Fortunately for us land lubbers, these Jurassic-looking beasts are ungraceful out of the water and are only capable of running at 11mph, a speed most humans will find it easy to outpace. In the water, however, it's a very different story.

If you spot a crocodile watching you, remain calm, keep eye contact with it and slowly move backwards. If a crocodile is heading straight for you, don't take this as a bluff – unlike elephants, crocodiles don't do bluff.

In the James Bond film *Live and Let Die*, the villain Tee Hee (the tall, well-tailored gent with the bionic claw as an arm) leaves Bond on a three-metre island surrounded by hungry crocodiles and by way of advice says, 'There are, two ways to disable a crocodile: one is to take a pencil and jam it in the pressure hole behind its eye. The other is twice as simple, you just put your hand in its mouth and pull all its teeth out. Heh, heh.'

His suggestion that you gouge its peepers to mulch is sage advice. Anatomically, the only soft spot on a crocodile – or alligator's – armour-like exterior is its eyes and inside its mouth. Both these animals will clamp you in their jaws with an extraordinary bite power of 3,700 pounds per square inch (a tiger's, by comparison, is 1,000 psi, while the average dog's is 100 psi). Then they will try to subdue you with a 'death roll', in which you'll be rolled round and round like a ragdoll in a tumble dryer.

Tee Hee's second suggestion may sound like madness – after all, who puts their arm in the gullet of a monster with bacteria-ridden teeth, sharp as dinner knives? However, there is a flap of skin behind the croc/gator's tongue called the palatal valve, which stops water going down its throat when its mouth is open underwater. If you happen to be in reaching distance, grab a hold of this flap and tug it open; the croc will immediately release you. If you're trying to rescue someone who is being attacked and you're in a boat, try to hit the croc on the head with an oar or anything you can use to get its attention.

Case Study: Survivors of croc attacks

In 2022, Bill Yan was in Australia's Northern Territory visiting a billabong for a Sunday afternoon fish. It was the end of the dry season and water levels were low, so it should have been easy to spot crocodiles in the water. As he followed a game trail towards the billabong, straight across it coming from the direction of the water and heading into some bushes was the tell-tale belly slide (path) of a saltwater crocodile, but since there were footprints imprinted over the top of it he figured it was an old slide. Suddenly, from the bush, an enormous 3.5-metre croc came flying at him. Yan quickly climbed a paper tree, shimmying out of range of the salty's jaws. It waited patiently glowering up at him, but the fisherman kept throwing bits of bark at it and after a while it had had enough and eventually shuffled off back into the billabong.

There's also the story of a fly fisherman from Queensland who was focusing on a bull, which was in the way of where he wanted to cast his line. As he was shooing it away, a saltwater crocodile bulleted out of the water and knocked him over. Its jaws fastened around his leg and despite his best attempts to hold onto a mangrove tree, the creature was just too strong and it began dragging him down the bank. The fisherman knew that if it got him into the water, it would take him into a death roll and that would be the end of him, lights out. Fortunately, he had the presence of mind to grab his pocketknife and repeatedly stabbed the reptile in its head. It let go of him just at the edge of the water.

Attacks in Queensland have recently increased to the extent that the local authorities are considering allowing the hunting of crocodiles in this area.

Shark attacks

The shark is a much-maligned, misunderstood creature and Peter Benchley, the long-deceased author of the novel and adapted film *Jaws*, has a lot to answer for as that film tapped into a primal fear that we all have about something seizing us when we are swimming out of our depth. According to *National Geographic*, 'the fear of being attacked by a shark is more about our emotional response than the reality.' Shark attacks and human mortalities occur because sharks often mistake surfers for seals. Given the choice, a shark would much rather eat a seal than a human being; most human interactions with great white sharks involve the creature taking a test nibble of them and then, having discovered there's not much meat, discarding the human.

Great white sharks are the world's largest carnivorous fish and have been known to grow up to 6.4 metres long. The female is much larger than the male. Your chances of being attacked by one are incredibly rare but that said, it does happen. Between 2014 and 2018, there was an average of 84 attacks and 4 deaths per year globally. Whites are found all over the world, as are bull sharks and tiger sharks. Tiger sharks are most likely to attack a human unprovoked.

Sharks are most active at dusk, night and dawn. You often find them where a river mouth meets the sea, or where the shelf of the seabed drops off into deep water. If you see fish leaping from the water and birds diving, there's a good chance that a shark is in the vicinity. If a shark is following you, slowly move towards a boat or the shoreline but don't splash and make lots of unnecessary movements as thrashing attracts the shark's interest. If you're diving, it may be best to dive down to the bottom and find cover until the shark has gone. If you find yourself with an aggressive shark, keep it in sight. Don't swim away from it as you may trigger its hunter instinct. If it makes a curious pass at you, hit it on the nose with a bunched fist to deter it, as this is the nerve centre. And if it comes back for another round, go for its eyes or rip at its gills, as these are the only vulnerable areas on the shark.

Sharks rarely attack a group of surfers or swimmers, preferring to go for lone targets. They are naturally drawn to blood - even a drop can be detected from a mile away by the creature's olfactory system. So, if you have an open wound, it's a bad idea to go swimming in waters where you might attract unwanted attention.

Case Study: Great white survivor Nick Fanning

In 2015, Australian surfing legend and world champion Nick Fanning was competing in a surf contest in Jeffries Bay, South Africa, when he was attacked and dragged under the water by a three-metre great white. The surfer was cool-headed enough to fight back with measured aim at the fish's gills and back and managed to drive his assailant away. Amazingly, he then stopped swimming for the shoreline and realised he needed to face the shark in case it came back before he was picked up by a jet ski support driver.

Hippo attacks

Forget all those Disneyfied images of cute-looking hippos, the reality is they are the deadliest large land mammal on Earth, killing some 500 people a year in Africa. With their 50-centimetre canine teeth and immense weight (around

1,500kg), these intimidating creatures are usually 3–4 metres in length. Big males can weigh almost two tons. These hooved killers might look ungainly, but they can swim faster than us and on land, they can reach speeds of 20mph. The average human running for their life clocks 12mph.

Hippos sleep during the day, submerging their body and sensitive skin under the water. By night, they leave the water to forage and feed as much as a mile inland. The hippopotamus is infamous for its volatile temper and impressive bite power. These animals are highly reactive to perceived incursions into their territory.

There's something very disturbing about being in a boat watching a pod of hippos and seeing the alpha male studying you with diabolical black eyes, then lunging forward and out of sight underwater, to come under the boat and try and flip it in order to get to you. In the rare event that it succeeds, as much as possible try to avoid splashing, as this will just draw the hippo towards you. Take a big deep breath, swim to the bottom and do your best to get to the nearest bank.

Case Study: Swallowed by a monster

In 1996, Paul Templar, a canoe safari guide in Zimbabwe, Southern Africa, was twice almost swallowed alive by a hippo on the Zambezi River. When another guide who was supposed to be leading the canoe safari came down with malaria, Templar stepped in. All was going well until they came across a pod of about a dozen hippos. Somebody asked if it was true that hippos killed 500 people a year in Africa. Templar admitted it was true and then suggested that they move on. There were seven canoes and suddenly Templar's was knocked off-course by a giant bull hippo. Meanwhile, one of the junior guides was made airborne and thrown into the river.

Templar told his clients to paddle back to safety while he paddled over to rescue the guide. As he reached down to pull him out of the water, it exploded with activity. He was suddenly somewhere deep, dark and dank and he was trying to move his arms but he couldn't; he realised he was headfirst up to his waist down a hippo's throat. Templar describes it as feeling slimy, slippery and wet, and smelling like a rotten egg. He grabbed hold of its tusks and managed to push himself out of its jaws and up to the surface for air.

There, he spotted the junior guide and swam over to help him. Once again, he found himself swallowed by the hippo, his legs dangling out of its mouth as it thrashed around. It tossed him up into the air and caught him in its mouth. When it bit down on him, Templar thought he was going to be chopped in half. He had an idea and that was to hang onto the hippo's tusks with each hand so that they couldn't bite through him again. Eventually the animal spat him out, having already pierced his lung and neck. Templar had 38 major bite wounds and his left arm from the elbow down had been crushed to a pulp.

Chimpanzee attacks

Well, this one is close to my heart. Of all the great apes – orangutan, gorilla, bonobo, human and chimpanzee – the chimpanzee is by far the most aggressive and sadly, the most like humans in their level of violence. According to a 2017 study published in the journal *PNAS*, chimpanzees are 1.35 times stronger than a strong human and have twice the amount of 'fast-twitch' muscle fibres as we do. When it comes to pushing, pulling and lifting, humans are weaker than apes. That arsenal of teeth with those enormous canines are not for show: chimps are built for the kill. Sarah Bell, science communicator at Oxford University Museum of Natural History, said, 'Anyone who has ever actually observed fully grown chimpanzees would never assume they could "take on" a chimpanzee. Chimpanzees have been known to tear off people's faces and leave men with a little less manhood than they had before the encounter.'

According to the *Harvard Gazette*, our closest relatives are similar to us humans in so far as they form tightly-knit social groups, engage in play and use tools to assist in catching their food. Back in the 1970s, when tea adverts for the brand PG Tips featuring chimps dressed as humans were at their height in the UK, nobody knew just how violent these animals could be. Attacks like the one on me, and more research performed in the wild, made zoologists realise just how wrong they had been about our cuddly friends. In the wild, chimpanzees engage in tribal warfare, regularly kill males, eat newborn babies and mutilate the corpses of former exiled group leaders. They even get drunk by sucking alcohol from fig trees.

Chimps move on all fours much quicker than we do and they're built for sprints. And yet, asked how they might fare in an intraspecies scrap, 17 per cent of Americans believed they could win a bare-knuckle brawl with a chimpanzee; 15 per cent believed they could win a fight with a king cobra, while 6 per cent of people believed they could beat a grizzly bear. Delusions of grandeur or what!

Among primates, showing your teeth held together is a signal of submission. The animal is only attacking because it feels threatened, so letting it know it has won is a good idea. Though make sure you don't let your mouth hang open while smiling as this shows a direct intention on your part, to attack. Clench your teeth together and bare them.

Chimps may be faster and stronger than we are because their bodies have more fast-twitch muscle fibres, but humans' slow-twitch muscle fibres are more fatigue resistant, which means we can keep running at an even pace for longer. A chimp will catch you in a sprint but if you can evade it and keep moving, you'll outrun it. However, if you see a body of water, run and jump in it. Chimps can't swim because their high muscle density prohibits buoyancy.

Case Study: Definitely not man's best friend

In captivity, chimpanzees can be much larger since they eat more and are less active. Males in captivity reach up to 80kg, females 68kg.

In 2009, Charlotte Nash went to see her friend Sandy, who owned a 14-year-old Chimp named Travis. As soon as Charlotte got out of her car, Travis knocked her to the ground and started tearing at her face. Charlotte's friend tried to stop him, but nothing worked. By the time the police arrived and shot the chimp dead, Charlotte had lost both hands and needed a face transplant.

The most lethal thing in a chimp's toolkit for violence is its intelligence, closely followed by its teeth. Avoid using your hands as a weapon; a chimp will simply seize your arm and bite your fingers off. Chimps also seem to know where your vital organs are.

Case Study: The giant Bili apes of the Congo

The hierarchy of chimps usually puts the larger, most dominant male at the top. Standing upright, chimps measure around 1–1.7 metres tall. Because they have long arms and short legs, chimps walk on all fours.

Imagine the excitement when stories began to filter back from the Bili forest in the Democratic Republic of Congo that a troupe of giant chimpanzees existed there so strong and large that they could take down lions.

Because the country has long been at war, it wasn't until recently that scientists were able to enter the deep, remote jungle to verify these accounts. They found that these super-sized apes really do exist and have certain similarities with gorillas. For instance, they nest on the ground as well as in the trees. They are also not scared of humans but instead show curiosity. Unlike their smaller cousins from the East Congo, they stand up to 2 metres tall and often walk upright on their hind legs. They also have a prominent brow ridge above the eyes like that of a gorilla.

The behaviour of these giant apes also differentiates itself from regular chimpanzees in the way that the females of the tribe tend to influence the males; they also engage in copulation as a way of soothing difficult situations. Much less aggressive than their smaller counterpart, the Bili ape is bisexual and has a grey face.

VICIOUS DOG ATTACKS

I believe vicious people are drawn towards dogs with a high prey drive. They then exploit this trait with rough and unsociable treatment of the animal, bringing it up with fear and habituating it to violence and pain so it knows no different. A dog isn't born bad, it's how it's treated which dictates how it acts. Some breeds will become aggressive more quickly than others.

There are currently 12 million dogs in the UK. In 2020, 1,700 children were injured by savage dogs, mainly with bites to the head. Nine people died from dog-bite attacks and a further 2,925 needed reconstructive surgery because of the injuries sustained. Disturbingly, there has been a staggering 26 per cent rise in dog bites since 2020.

It's interesting that of all fatal dog attacks in the US, 56 per cent were committed by pit bulls. Since the 1990s, fatal dog attacks have almost doubled. Maybe it's the owners we need to start locking up.

Never run from a dog you think is about to attack you because this will trigger their prey drive. Stand still, cross your arms on your chest and show no sign of fear. This will throw them off balance. Calmly ask for help from any passers-by. Never scream, even if the animal starts fighting you, as this will only agitate and escalate things further. Don't make direct eye contact with the dog as this could be seen as a challenge. Remain still and eventually the dog will lose interest and walk off. Standing still is easier said than done; if you're not protecting a child or another dog and there's a tree nearby, get your ass up it as quickly as possible. Pit bulls can jump two metres into the air, so that gives you an idea of how far you must climb. If there's no tree, climb on top of the car, and if there's no car, any weapon from a stick to an umbrella is better than nothing.

If a dog clamps its jaws on you and won't let go, you could try strangling the animal with your free arm around its throat. Or if possible, you can yank its front legs apart to break its knees. Gouge the animal's eyes or push your umbrella up its rectum. Blocking an attacking dog's vision has a sudden effect of making them let go of you. In the US, they use pepper spray or mace to distract and temporarily blind attacking dogs. But in the UK, both are illegal. The legal equivalent is 'Farbgel' self-defence spray.

If your dog is attacked by another dog, don't try to separate them as you can end up being bitten too. If your child is attacked, throwing cold water over the animal can be an effective way of breaking its primal circuit and shocking it so it stops, or grab its rear legs and pull them as far apart as you can. There is no penalty for taking a dog's life who is attacking your child or another person.

Dog breeds to be wary of

A common saying familiar to nurses stitching up kids attacked by the family fido is, 'He's never done that before.' It's not just unknown dogs that attack, often it happens in the house. But much of it is to do with the breed of the animal as well as the way it is treated. The usual suspect breeds seem to pop up again and again, and they are generally dogs that were originally bred to guard and fight.

The American pit bull is statistically one of the most dangerous dogs and the dog most likely to turn on its owner. Once they clamp down on you with those impressively powerful jaws, they won't let go. The pit bull then shakes its victim like a ragdoll and children just don't stand a chance. In the US, 34 per cent of attacks on humans were carried out by pit bulls and of these 66 per cent were fatal.

- **Rottweiler.** It's not just because they featured in *The Omen* and scared the bejesus out of us all. Rotties weigh up to 60kg and can stand 70 centimetres at the shoulder. They have appeared in more dog- bite statistics than any other dog. They are highly protective dogs and said to be very affectionate at home with their human pack but become anxious when separated or left alone.
- **Dogo Argentino.** Bred from mastiffs, this highly aggressive breed is regarded as being so dangerous that it is banned in many countries, including Norway, Denmark, Malaysia, Australia, Ukraine and the UK.
- **Boerboel.** Bred from a mastiff and a bulldog, they were used to hunt lions in Africa. This massive dog can weigh up to 80kg. They should not be around children.
- **Kangal.** This huge livestock guard dog has been selectively bred over hundreds of years to protect sheep from wolves. Consistently voted the most dangerous dog on the planet, it can jump onto a two-metre-high fence and run an impressive 31mph. It has the strongest bite power of all dogs and will die for their flock.
- **Akita.** These Japanese fighting dogs are becoming a common sight in parks across the UK. Incredibly

strong-willed and independent, they are definitely not a dog for beginners. They require constant handling as their dominant personality wants them to become the pack leader. They are also aggressive towards other dogs and people. An akita is also very territorial over their food and children should never go near them if they're eating.

- **Perro de Presa Canario.** This dog has an exceedingly high prey drive and can attack without warning. It's suspicious of strangers and other dogs. Headstrong and energised, they are difficult dogs to handle.
- **Tosa Inu.** Bred in Japan to fight without making a noise and often turn on their owners.
- **Cane Corso.** Bred for hunting boars and mountain lions, they stand around 65cm tall to their shoulder. Used in dog fighting.
- **Doberman.** Bred to intimidate, they are banned in 16 US states.
- **Caucasian shepherd dog.** Used to guard sheep against wolves and bears, they were also used in Russian prisons to pursue escaping convicts. Highly dominant.

PART SIX:

THE BREAKDOWN OF SOCIETY

SOCIETAL BREAKDOWN

According to a story in the *Guardian* newspaper in 2022, almost half of Americans interviewed feared their country would erupt into civil war over the coming decade, predicting a dystopian nightmare. When Donald Trump's Florida home was raided by the FBI in 2022, references on Twitter to'civil war' jumped by 3,000 per cent.

The article points to two major factors which put a country at risk of civil war are 'ethnic factionalism', when citizens organise their political parties according to their religious or racial identity rather than political beliefs, and something called 'anocracy' (yep, I've never heard of it either). This is when a country is neither democratic nor dictatorial, but a hybrid of the two, that appears to allow minor opposition but in reality the incumbent government has complete control. Governments like this are susceptible to pockets of resistance and outbreaks of armed conflict.

The Arab Spring of 2010–12 was a wave of political protests against corruption, which in some cases escalated to armed rebellions and even civil war. Starting in Tunisia, it spread across much of the Middle East, including countries like Libya, Iran, Yemen, Syria, Egypt, Morocco, Jordan and Bahrain. In a high number of cases but not all, these demonstrations lead to an increase in violence and human rights abuse committed by governments attempting to stymie political change.

My point – just in case you're wondering what that little history lesson was all about – is to give you some context of how quickly a society can become polarised and a civil war can flare up. Here in the UK, day-to-day commodities like foodstuffs, mortgages, rent, fuel for our cars and heating our houses have become increasingly expensive – all things which until recently many of us took for granted. When rates of severe poverty increase, ordinary people may feel forced by these extreme circumstances to do extraordinary things they wouldn't usually dream of. Like stealing wood from a neighbour's garden, shoplifting, syphoning fuel from someone else's car – maybe even threatening violence in order to get what's needed to heat their home or feed their family. To protect our kin from danger, be it to people who pose a threat to them, hunger, severe weather, illness, etc., we are prepared to do things we wouldn't otherwise. Certainly, there comes a point at which if we believe the law is unfair or no longer representing us, we take justice into our own hands. Desperate people take desperate measures.

A recent NASA-backed study considering previous history and firmly rooted in scientific data predicted a slowly spiralling downward course for humanity rather than the sudden fireworks of a nuclear war. The study identified certain key factors that could cause the collapse of civilisation, like badly handled climate change which then affects water, agriculture and energy supplies. And gradual ecological breakdown, where extreme weather becomes the norm, with flooding, drought, rising temperatures and increasing ocean levels, as well as intolerable UV levels caused by deforestation and an excess of carbon dioxide being released, all slowly leading us into chaos. The study concluded that society would eventually consume more than it had with only the rich having access to vital resources, leading to total collapse.

In his book, *The Knowledge: How to Rebuild Our World from Scratch*, Professor Lewis Darnell lists empires and details how long they endured before they self-destructed as a result of the growing gulf between rich and poor, political corruption and decadence. He cites cultures as diverse as the empires of Persia, Ottoman, Greece, Rome and England to back up this claim. The mean average of their existence is around 240 years.

If society collapses, then the maintenance of power stations will cease and the grid will go down rapidly, leading to the internet, now no longer supported by its servers, collapsing entirely. Regular tech that we depend on, like mobile phones and GPS, will also be lost. That's when your neighbour becomes a stranger and a competitor for a limited supply of vital resources like food and water.

How to plan for societal breakdown

The only way to survive when common sense in your society goes completely AWOL is to prepare for it and that starts with getting organised now and not putting it off until tomorrow. Be aware that famine is not only caused by a lack of food but also by an inability to access it. If power supplies are switched off, you'll need gas or solar power generators to maintain heating and lighting. If you live in an area which suffers severe winters, make sure your home is as insulated as possible. Get comfortable building fires in a few minutes – a woodstove will allow you to heat your house and also cook your dinner.

The Vikings could never have discovered America, 500 years ahead of Christopher Columbus, if it hadn't been for the fact that they carried dried cod with them on their long voyages. In the absence of salt, they used to dry fresh cod on racks in the salty air. Today, salt is still important because of its ability to preserve food. During the collapse of society, once fast food is no longer being made and it's much harder to refrigerate anything, salt will become a *very* precious commodity because of its ability to preserve freshly hunted meat and grown vegetables.

When trouble comes to your door

If rioting and looting breaks out, how are you going to protect your family? The answer is by expecting the worst and having a plan of action. If you're living in a city, predictive models suggest you're more vulnerable because the limited resources you depend on will be stretched across a disproportionately large amount of people. History has taught us that when too many humans are competing for the same thing, desperation breeds violence. In rural areas, you'd be able to grow your own food, have more access to water supplies and lower population density would mean less chances of attack, increasing the odds of your survival. Also, the benefit of more remote rural places to see out the societal collapse means fewer people will know what you're up to when you start preparing, as opposed to living in a city where it's much harder to stockpile.

Think logistically about it: do you have any family who live in remote rural areas and would they be prepared for you to come and live with them in the event of everything turning Mad Max?

But while the overpopulated cities may see neighbour pitted against neighbour and gangs roaming the streets, that doesn't mean you want to be completely isolated at this time. Communal strength will be more beneficial in the long term than being a lone wolf. You're much better off establishing bonds with other people who you can work with and learn to trust, rather than facing lawlessness alone. The formation of your group depends on shared values, equality and fair play, with someone you believe in who can provide decent leadership. As a solo operator, however, working alone depending on nobody but yourself, not only are you vulnerable with no backup, but there's no one with whom to share your worries, take care of you if you're ill and keep you human.

A good team is made up of diverse talents and different personalities. Some people will bring strength, wisdom and humour, others vision and practicality, quickly falling into the right roles where they can best contribute. Much as they are the stuff of fiction, TV series like the *Walking Dead* offer an insight into how easily some tribes, when led by the wrong leaders, lose those essential qualities which make us human and quickly descend into cannibalism and murder, while others seek to retain their social values and hold fast to their humanity.

The academic and author Nafeez Ahmed, who studies global crises, societal collapse and mass violence, suggests that when a government's only option to control anarchy is introducing martial law (when the army takes control), citizens should never trust them 100 per cent. He adds, 'You don't necessarily have to be a conspiracy theorist to question authority. In the West, we know there is a certain degree of discipline and accountability that our military do have – there are rules of engagement. But we know from history that when you have this sort of situation, there is all sorts of scope for abuse.' Martial law involves a massive reduction in an individual's freedom, including your access to food medicine and energy to power your home. The best way to operate under these strict circumstances is to play the game and keep your head down, not getting noticed by the authorities. Expect roadblocks, checkpoints and imposed curfews.

If the trouble is many miles away from where you live, you and your family can hunker down in your own house – keeping abreast of current affairs by using a wind-up radio

– and hope the violence won't spread. You'll also need to make sure you have a firearm to defend yourself and your family, food and water supplies and home. However, if supplies have been exhausted in the city and predators are starting to loot further afield in your area you will need to get out of your house quickly and ally yourself with other people if you haven't already done so.

Once you have found a group in which to protect yourself and your family, you are satisfying the third level of Maslow's hierarchy of needs (see pages 32–5), the feeling that you belong. But of equal importance are levels one and two – finding a credible shelter in which to stay safe and store your essential supplies, as well as getting enough sleep to function to the maximum. Next, you need to select a leader, as only through developing a sense of structure and control can you bring order to the unfolding chaos around you. The natural leaders in the group will make themselves known, then it is a case of picking the right one. Perhaps you can suggest a vote of confidence to help you choose.

Planning the route to your bug-out shelter

It's no great surprise that you will be avoiding major highways and motorways as others will be seeking to reach other destinations too. You have to ask yourself constantly what a normal person would think of doing and then do the opposite. Every Tom, Dick and Harriet will be jumping in the car and heading down the highway, only to find themselves half an hour later gridlocked in a huge pile-up of overheating cars, road rage, fear, screaming babies and people climbing out of their cars. And if it's a societal breakdown scenario, you'll be a sitting duck for predators. So, avoid major roads at all costs. Instead, look at a map and begin to design a route through back country. You should have more than one route in mind just in case a road is blocked and you must double back and seek an alternative. At any time, you must be prepared to abandon your vehicle and go on by foot. This is another consideration if you're travelling to a relative who lives a fair distance away. If society has broken down, is it realistic that you're going to make it that far?

When I choose a vehicle as my family car, it must offer more than a means of transport that looks nice and makes people see I'm doing well. I have vehicles with the ability to venture off the beaten track and one specific vehicle that could pretty much go over anything and provide the ability for life support for an extended period of time. It may be worth your consideration when choosing your next family vehicle.

Once you have planned your route to your bug-out shelter, you then need to physically drive each route and pick out landmarks that you will use as emergency rendezvous points. For instance, a grain tower or a folly on a hill; a lightning-struck tree or another easily detectable conspicuous landmark. Then, if your family gets split up, you will all know where to try to get yourselves to.

This might seem a little intimidating, but as recently as the 1990s, we didn't all have mobile phones and we usually had to make fallback plans. In this case, the plan might be: 'If we get separated, let's meet at 8 o'clock at such and such a place and remain in position for no less than an hour, repeating that window each day until we are reunited. . .' Your family need to be brought into this because it's going to take some time and effort if you're going to be prepared; they need to be in the car with you when you do a dummy drive and help you choose landmarks where you can meet, if necessary.

CHEMICAL OR BIOLOGICAL ATTACK

Of all the weapons of mass destruction, chemical warfare is probably one of the most brutal. The use of chemical materials by criminals and terrorist groups provides a significant threat to humans on a wide scale. In March 1995, Tokyo's subway system was hit by synchronised chemical attacks on five different trains, in which the military nerve agent sarin was released, killing 12 and injuring another 5,000. Terrorist entities like Al-Qaeda, ISIS and Hamas are all alleged to have used chemical weapons in their warfare.

Extracting toxic chemicals from plant extracts to poison individuals is nothing new, in fact it goes back as far as the Middle Ages. But it wasn't until the Industrial Revolution in the nineteenth century when mass deployment of chemical warfare agents became a real prospect. Chemical warfare was first introduced in a German gas attack in 1915 at Ypres in Belgium, during the First World War.

Terrorists use chemical and biological weapons because they're relatively cheap, easy to transport and can be used against entire populations. In 2001, powdered anthrax spores were deliberately put into letters that were mailed through the US postal system. Twenty-two people, including 12 mail handlers, were poisoned with anthrax and five of those died. Chemical and biological weapons inspire dread and fear, which is the precise aim of a terrorist. Chemical and biological attacks are similar in that they use barely visible chemicals or organisms that can make you sick or even kill you.

Different kinds of chemical attack:

- Phosphene
- Cyanide
- Mustard gas
- Nerve agents (like sarin)
- Riot control agents (like Mace)
- Incapacitating agents.

Biological agents used in attacks:

- Bacteria – organisms that can be treated with toxins that replicate on their own
- Viruses – needs a host to replicate
- Toxins – poisons extracted from animals.

Biological agents can be delivered by infecting livestock and letting them spread the poison, and through food and water.

Signs that somebody has been exposed to a chemical and biological attack:

- unexplained signs of skin, eye or airways irritation
- nausea and vomiting
- twitching
- sweating
- disorientation
- breathing difficulties
- odd smells or tastes
- blistering
- choking
- coughing up blood.

Steps to take if you think you are the victim of a chemical/biological attack:

- Remove all clothing and wash your body with soap and water to physically remove the contaminant, but don't scrub or press the skin as the pathogen will be absorbed into your skin
- Take everything you've come into contact with (without touching it with your naked hands) –

phone, keys, clothes, etc. – bag them, drive to the most depopulated area in your surroundings and burn it all

- Be careful helping others as you might expose yourself to contamination
- Wash your eyeglasses in bleach and rinse them afterwards
- Flush your eyes with water.

Your disaster supply kit for a biological or chemical attack should include:

- first aid kit
- plastic sheeting for windows and doors
- duct tape and scissors
- plenty of food and drinking water
- a sanitation kit, including soap and bleach
- radio for receiving government updates
- Torch.

Controlling your environment:

- By staying at home you can control your environment, such as by switching off the air conditioning and closing vents
- Shelter in the room with the least windows, sealing up the cracks in the doorframe and windows with duct tape and plastic sheeting

- Everyone in the room needs three square metres of floor space for five hours of air
- Use an alcohol-based disinfectant to clean your hands on a regular basis
- Avoid exposure to infected people
- Exercise social distancing
- Stay at home to work and keep your kids off school
- Wear a mask as the virus can be spread through the air
- Keep a small amount of cash at home in case the banks shut
- Stock up on food and water supplies.

POST-NUCLEAR WAR

The Cuban Missile Crisis of 1962 almost plunged the world into nuclear darkness after an American U-2 spy plane photographed missile installations being secretly installed on the island of Cuba by the Soviet Union. What followed was a face-off between the then US president, John F Kennedy, and Russian premier, Nikita Khrushchev. Soviet ships carrying nuclear missiles bound for Cuba were held back by a US nautical blockade of the island. When the Soviet ships altered their course and began to sail away from the quarantine area still intent on reaching

Cuba the tension ratcheted up to impossible levels before Khrushchev capitulated, agreeing to remove their missiles from Cuba, while Kennedy committed to the US never invading Cuba. This was the closest the world had come to a nuclear war.

Compared to then, the world is now an even more dangerous and volatile place, with NATO treading a tightrope of deterrence and diplomacy with modern-day Russia like never before. Back in the early 1960s, at least the Soviet leader could lay claim to being a relatively sane human being, while Kennedy was one of the best presidents the US has ever had.

There are now nine countries in possession of nuclear warheads. Even compared to the Cuban Missile Crisis of 1962, military analysts believe there is now a higher probability of a nuclear war occurring in our lifetime. Those of us who grew up in the 1960s and 70s lived in the constant shadow of the spectre of nuclear war between the superpowers and now it has returned. It's not just the business magnate Elon Musk who believes that the 'nuclear war probability is rising', the Doomsday clock, which measures the threat of a nuclear Ragnarok, is currently at 100 seconds to midnight, or on 'doom's doorstep'.

The best countries to be in in the event of a global nuclear war

Iceland, Australia, New Zealand, Norway, Sweden, Fiji and Greenland all make the list, thanks to their isolated locations, neutrality and relatively small populations in relation to the size of their landmass. They also don't have a military presence, which would oblige them to be pulled into the conflict. Easter Island is said to be so far from any other country in the Pacific that the nuclear fallout would not reach its shores, but how the hell are you going to get *there* in a hurry? Other contenders include Antarctica but there's not much infrastructural appeal here for those looking to start a new life.

For those of you closer in mainland UK, the most obvious target for a nuclear attack would be London and its surrounding suburbs, home to 12 million people. Secondary targets would be locations like GCHQ near Gloucester and Cheltenham, as it's the home of the UK's intelligence, security and cyber protection. Given that the thermal radiation radius of a nuclear blast is 12,960km^2, there are a few places in the country that lie beyond this radius, like the Shetland Isles in Scotland. Realistically, in the event of a bomb making its way to London or Gloucester, most of us are not going to be able to reach these isolated isles.

LinkedIn founder Reid Hoffman told the *New Yorker* that around 50 per cent of Silicon Valley's billionaires have 'apocalypse insurance', a term describing the high-luxe doomsday bunkers they've had built in New Zealand. This remote country has become a mecca for seriously minted Californian preppers. The big question is whether you want to survive long enough to live in a post-apocalyptic landscape. What's waiting for you will not be pretty.

What will happen if a nuclear bomb is launched?

According to Nuke Map (nuclearsecrecy.com/nukemap), if the strongest nuclear missile the US currently possesses was, for example, dropped on central London, around 700,000 people would be killed, with over 1 million injured. The blast range would cover Croydon and travel well into Surrey, while east and north London would be incinerated, as would much of Essex. Goodbye, Ant Middleton!

Given that a nuclear bomb reaches top speed around ten minutes after launch, a missile fired from Russia aimed at London would take about 20 minutes to reach Britain, giving us very little time to get ourselves organised and find somewhere to hide which is sufficiently protected from the initial blast and subsequent fallout. Strangely, here in the UK, we don't actually have a nuclear warning system at the moment. One was scheduled to have been finished by October 2022, but I understand that, at time of writing, it is still being tested. The UK's government website suggests it will work like a radio broadcast in an emergency: 'mobile phone masts in the surrounding area will broadcast the alert and every compatible mobile phone or tablet in range of a mast will receive the alert by text.'

Until this new warning system surfaces, all is not lost. RAF Fylingdales, a military station in North Yorkshire, gives warnings for the UK and the US, which, according to the *Daily Express* 'ensure[s] a surprise missile attack cannot succeed'. The station, which with its domed tents looks like something out of *The X*-Files, claims to have the ability to track objects up to 3,000 miles into space.

The original 'four-minute warning' system I grew up with, which was triggered by Jodrell Bank Observatory in Cheshire, could detect inbound missiles headed for the UK. It was used for 39 years between 1953 and 1992 and became obsolete at the end of the Cold War in 1991.

If a missile strikes your city

Phase one of a nuclear missile striking your city is a flash of super-intense light, followed by a fireball 2km across. Within its deathly perimeter, everything – buildings, cars, infrastructure, people – is reduced to a crisp. A heat pulse hotter than our sun will then radiate outward and incinerate everything within 13km of the detonation area. If you're within sight of the initial blast don't look at it, even from 20km, as you'll be temporarily blinded.

Twenty kilometres from the detonation site

As the bomb detonates and the electrical pulse radiates, it renders unshielded electronics instantly useless. So all cars relying on sophisticated electric software will no longer work. (Old bangers will be fine!) Personal computers, mobile phones, iPads, even pacemakers, within a 40-mile radius of the blast will also no longer function. The local power grid is now damaged beyond repair. After the white flash, fireball and the electromagnetic pulse have done their damage and you have about ten minutes to get out of the vicinity of the mushroom cloud before plumes of highly contaminated nuclear fallout start descending from the sky. Time, distance and shelter are the three factors which will decide whether you survive or not.

Ionising radiation is now attacking the city with radioactive dust. Trying to outrun the wind-borne dust is pointless, even if you're travelling at speed in a fast car, and it is covering everything. Anyone beneath the black stem of a mushroom cloud will be wiped out by it – the problem is the top of the mushroom that gets lifted on the wind and blown at speed.

How to prepare for a nuclear attack

Try to identify suitable underground places near where you work and live, and close to your children's school. Remember, the deeper underground you are, the safer you'll be from the fallout.

Emergency supply kit/get home bag for emergencies that happen whilst you're at work or away from home

- FFP2 respirators
- strong polythene bags
- gaffer tape
- rubber gloves
- potassium iodide pills (to help against radiation)
- radio receiver

- map and compass
- bottled water
- non-perishable food
- batteries (including spares) – vital for powering radios, which will be your source of updated info as the Web will be down
- medicine
- packaged food.

If you're in a car ...

Stay put in your vehicle. If you've got any duct tape, use it to seal all ventilation entry points into the car and check that the lining of the door is not ripped and that there's no way any dust can get through the engine bay into the car. So far, the car has kept you alive because it's absorbed the initial heat thrown out by the burning wave and now it's going to keep you safe from the radiation-charged dust touching your skin. Head for the hills if you can as contamination settles in valleys and low areas. Keeping upwind of the fallout contaminating the air is paramount.

If you can get inside a building ...

Better than a car, which won't protect you from radioactive fallout for long, is to try to shelter in the nearest suitable building, keeping away from the windows. A basement is best. If there are others gathered there, try to maintain a distance of at least two metres between you and them. If you still have a mask floating around in your bag from the Covid-19 pandemic, put it on. Seal all entry points into the room, including all windows and doors and the frame around the door, to stop the deadly dust getting into your immediate environment. As soon as possible, once indoors, remove your clothes, which will be carrying radiation, and shower yourself thoroughly. If you don't have a water supply, then use wet wipes. If you're starting to vomit the chances are you're already on your way to a visit from the Grim Reaper.

Find the metro

Better than a car or a building is to head to the nearest underground station (if there is one in your city) and descend as deeply as you can. Then sit tight for the next 24 hours. Eighty per cent of the fallout contamination's energy is lost within the first 48 hours but the threat of internal contamination is still very much a reality; radioactive dust will be ingested just by breathing in. Wear a wet cloth over your nose to prevent this. Your 'get home bag' that you've kept to hand for emergencies means that it's possible to survive down here for the next three days.

Head out of the city in the opposite direction of the wind. As soon as possible, get to your shelter or home. Hopefully you will have sufficiently prepped your water supplies – in the coming days it will be more valuable than money which will soon lose its currency. Outside, the world is still, everything covered in lethal grey radioactive dust. Search for a radio so you can hear any emergency news output, but don't dally – just being outside is bad for your health. Try to find allies, form a group. Now it's time to move away from the blast area as quickly as you can.

EPILOGUE

I heard Sylvester Stallone saying something the other day that really struck me; it was along the lines that he'd realised in his autumn years that there was now more runway behind him than left in front of him. Well into his seventies, 'Sly' Stallone is a true survivor and one who is managing to survive the piranhas, pikes and sharks of the Hollywood star system. At 76, he still works out and dishes out free life advice to anyone who needs it on Instagram. He's a walking cry against hanging up your gloves and dying in your slippers. Like me, he believes that it's how you think that dictates how old you feel, not the years that you've accumulated.

I've been blessed to have so far lived a colourful life full of adventure, but that's because I've sought it out rather than waited for it to come to me (though perhaps at times the wrong kind of adventure). You might question if I had a death wish, but for the most part I'm so grateful for the challenges that I have undertaken and have managed to survive and thrive through.

If you've never heard the soulful 'Whoop-whoop!' of a gibbon waking up the jungle at dawn, or you've never camped under the stars in the Arabian desert, it's all waiting for you. We're all brief visitors on this beautiful Earth and my hope is that you will seek out the best bits of it using this book to keep yourself safe in the process.

Enjoy!

Ollie Ollerton

INDEX